© Copyright 2024 - All rights reserved.

You may not reproduce, duplicate or send the contents of this book without direct written permission from the author. You cannot hereby despite any circumstance blame the publisher or hold him or her to legal responsibility for any reparation, compensations, or monetary forfeiture owing to the information included herein, either in a direct or an indirect way.

Legal Notice: This book has copyright protection. You can use the book for personal purposes. You should not sell, use, alter, distribute, quote, take excerpts, or paraphrase in part or whole the material contained in this book without obtaining the permission of the author first.

Disclaimer Notice: You must take note that the information in this document is for casual reading and entertainment purposes only. We have made every attempt to provide accurate, up-to-date, and reliable information. We do not express or imply guarantees of any kind. The persons who read admit that the writer is not occupied in giving legal, financial, medical, or other advice. We put this book content by sourcing various places.

Please consult a licensed professional before you try any techniques shown in this book. By going through this document, the book lover comes to an agreement that under no situation is the author accountable for any forfeiture, direct or indirect, which they may incur because of the use of material contained in this document, including, but not limited to, α errors, omissions, or inaccuracies.

THIS BOOK BELONGS TO

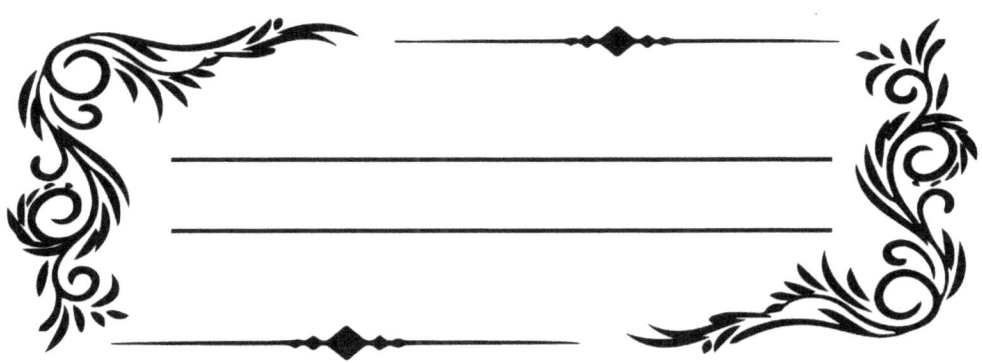

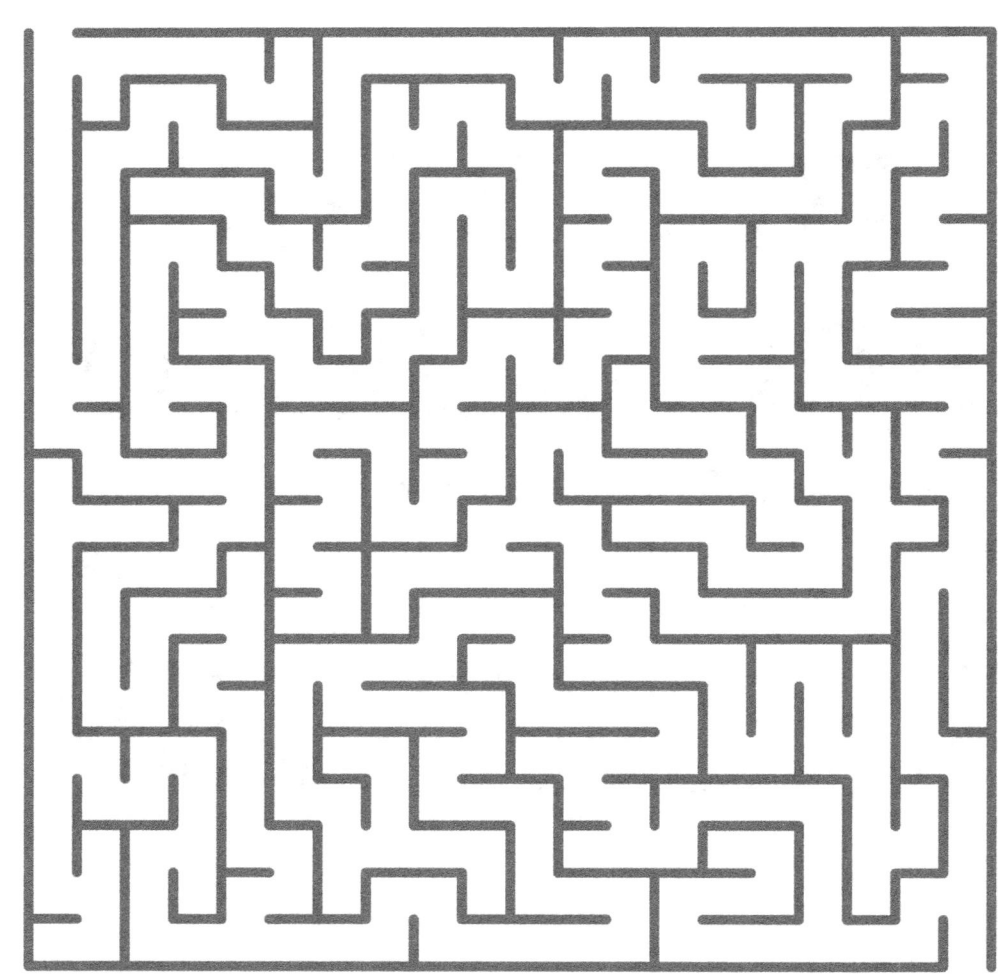

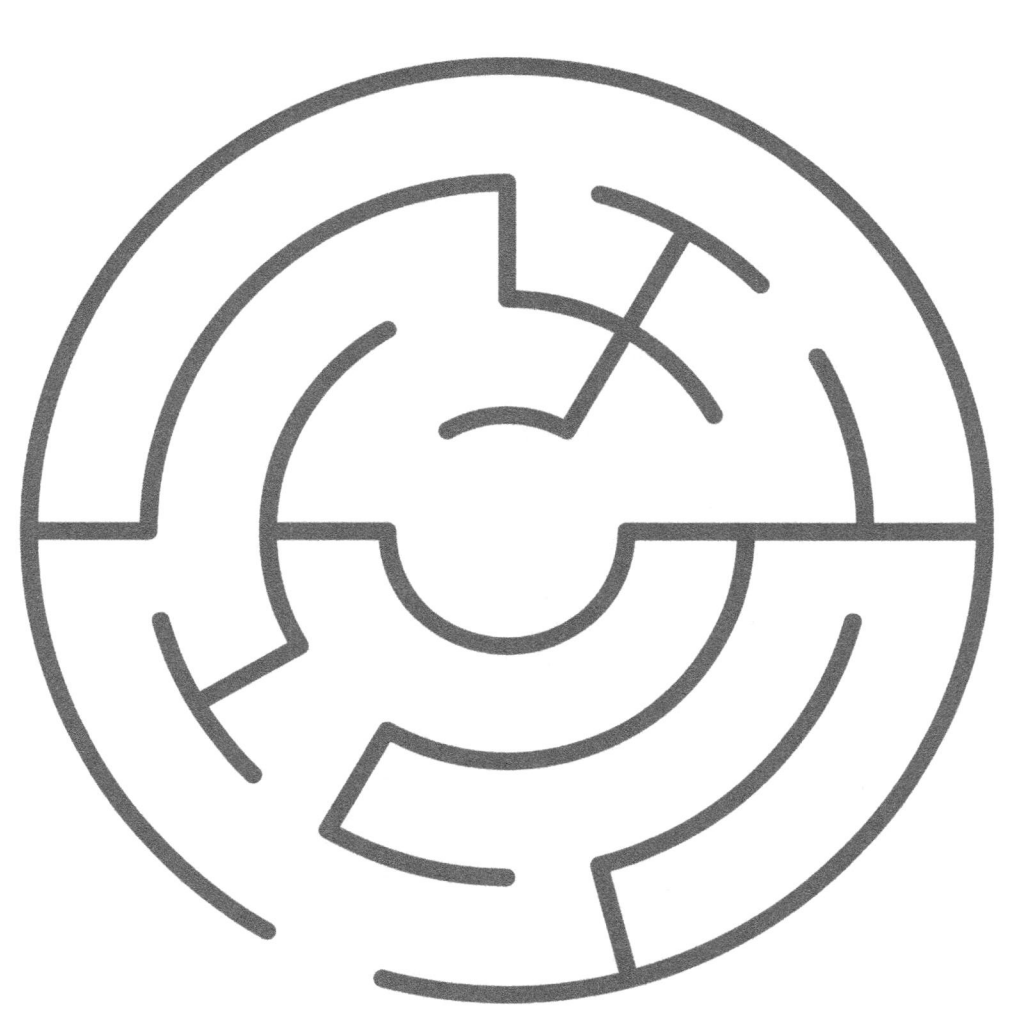

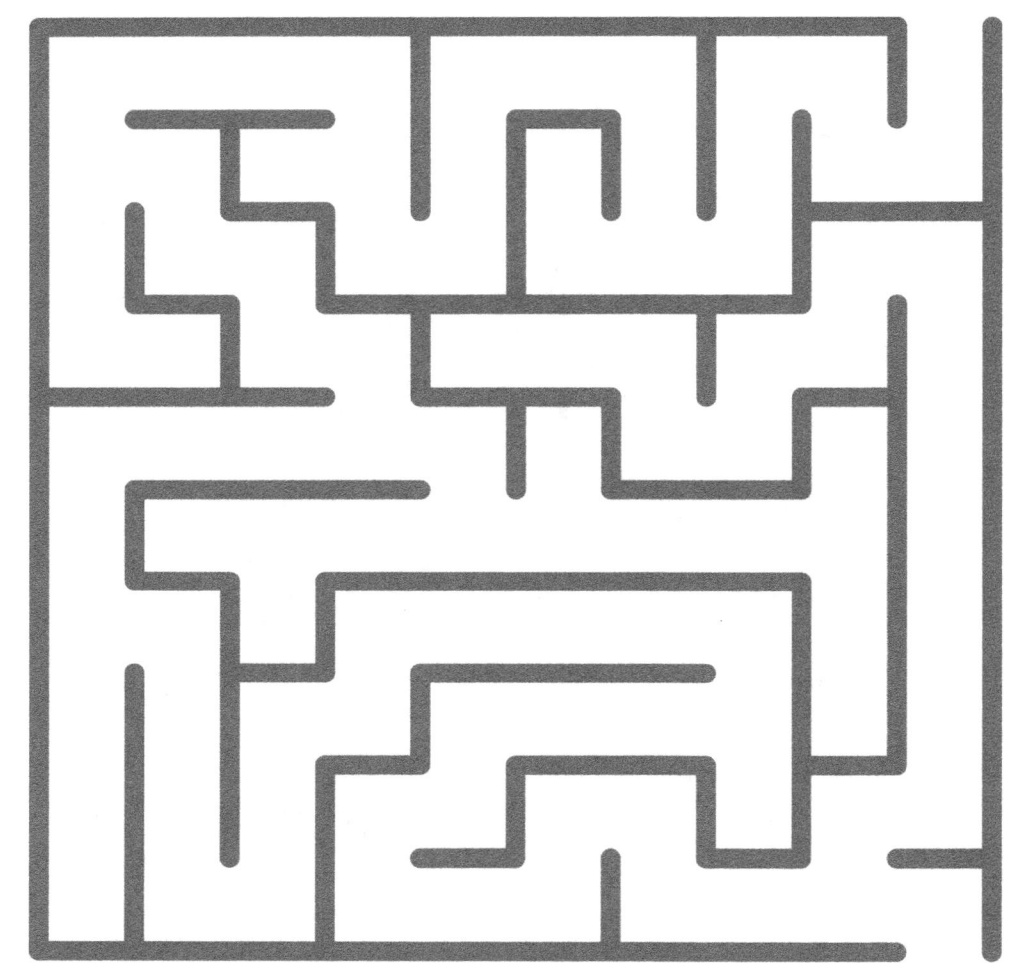

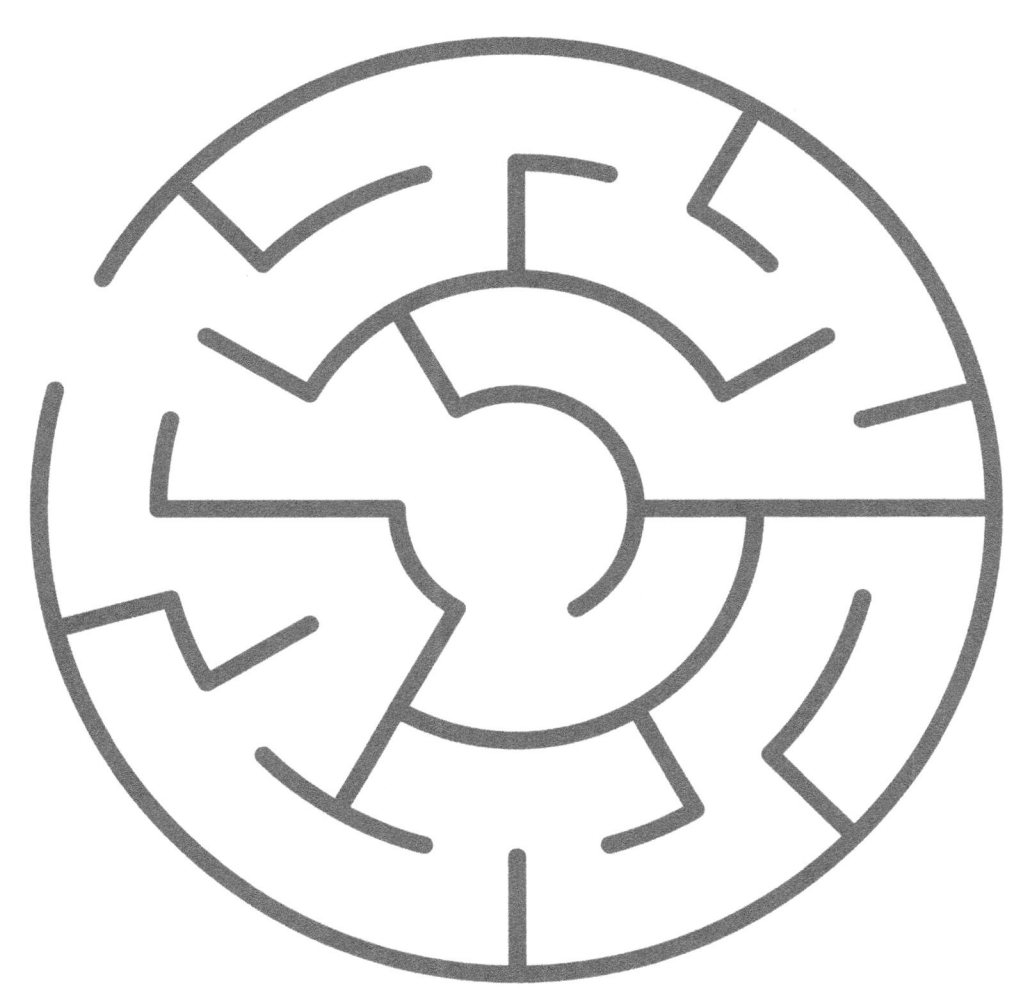

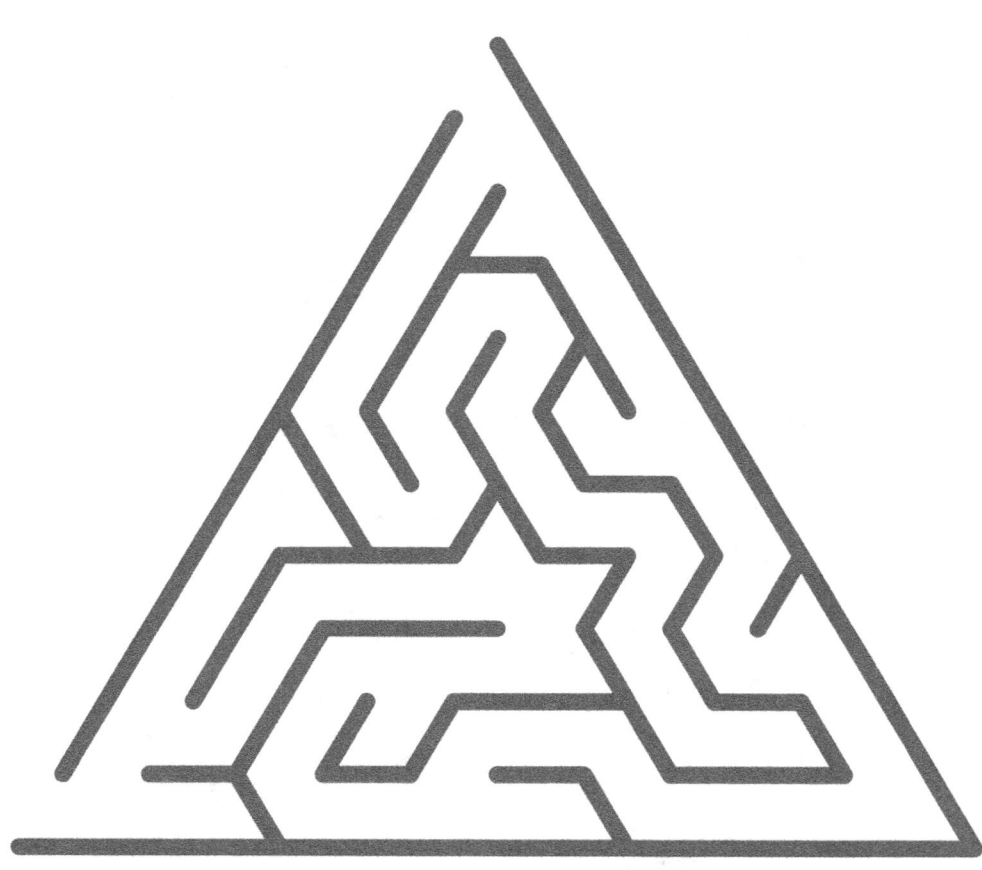

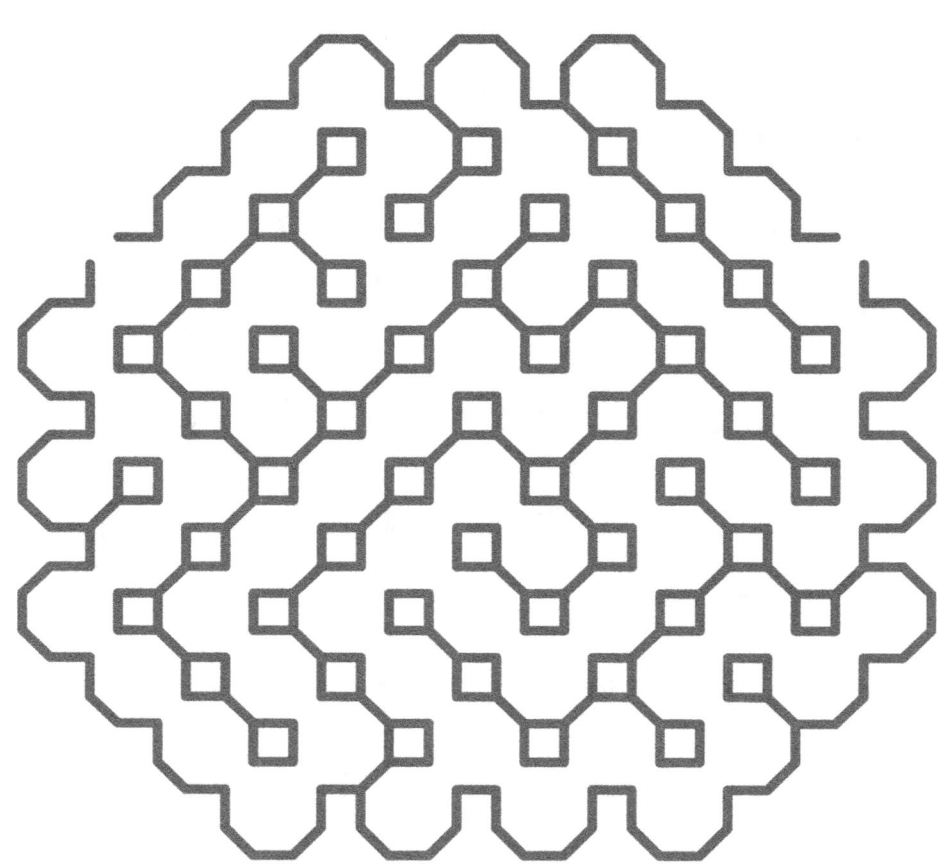

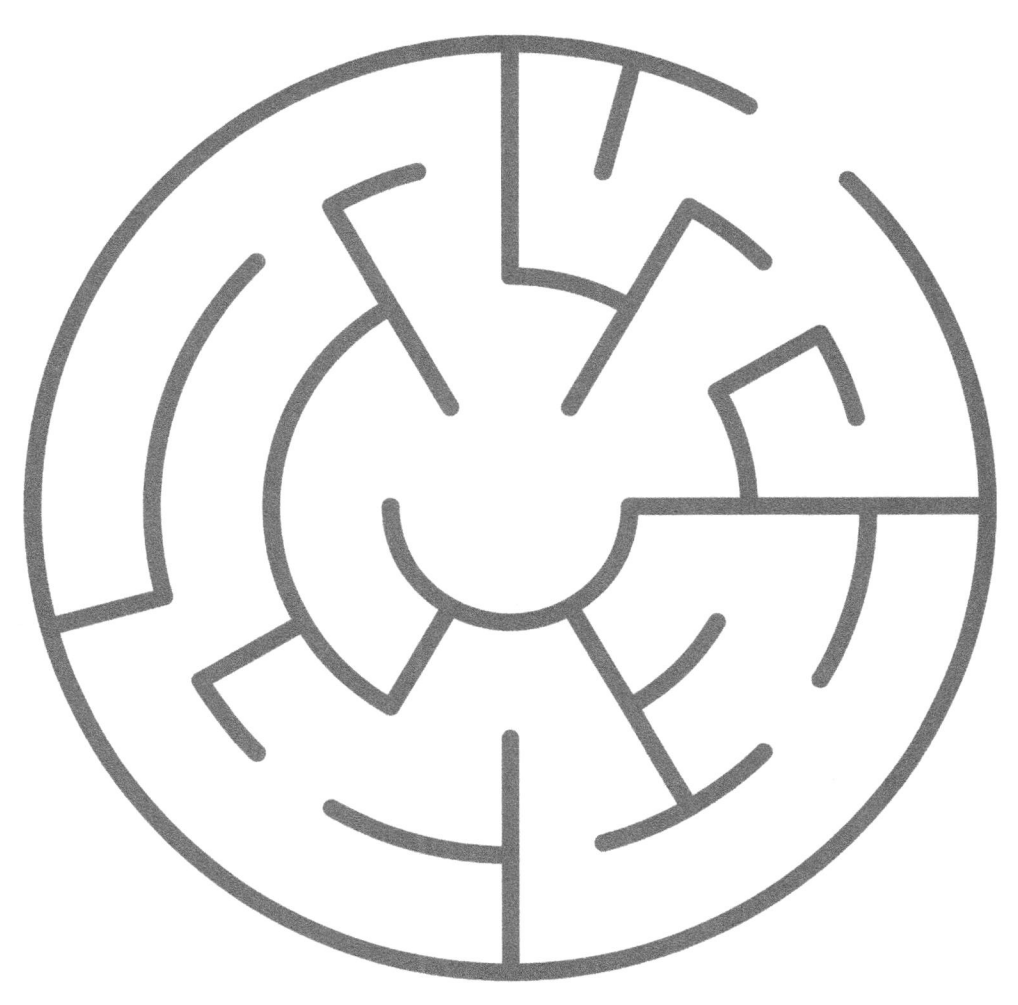

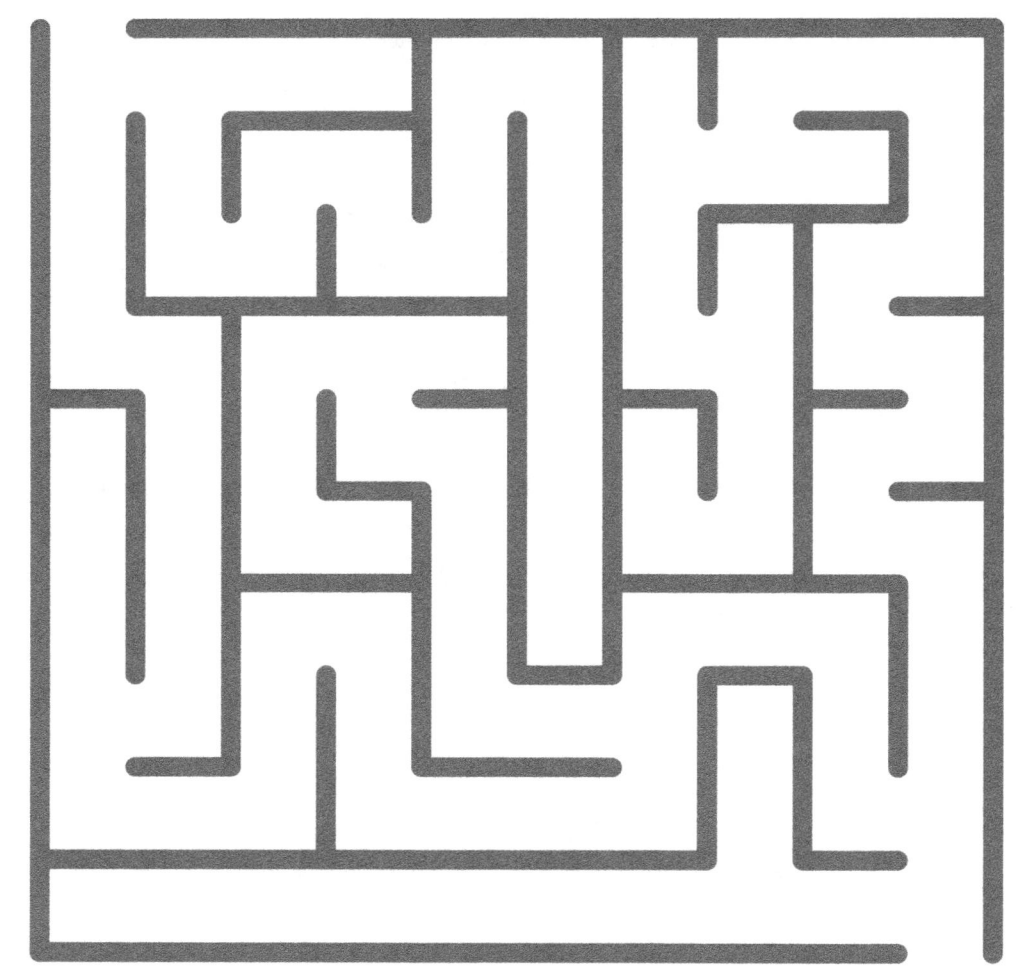

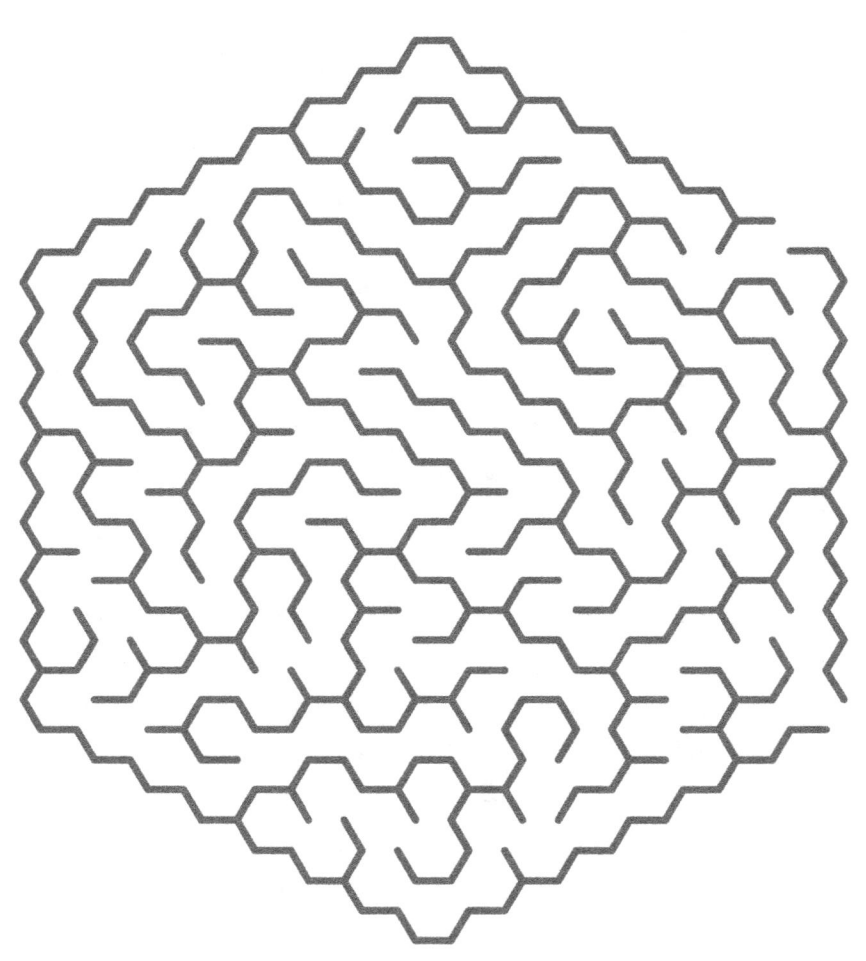

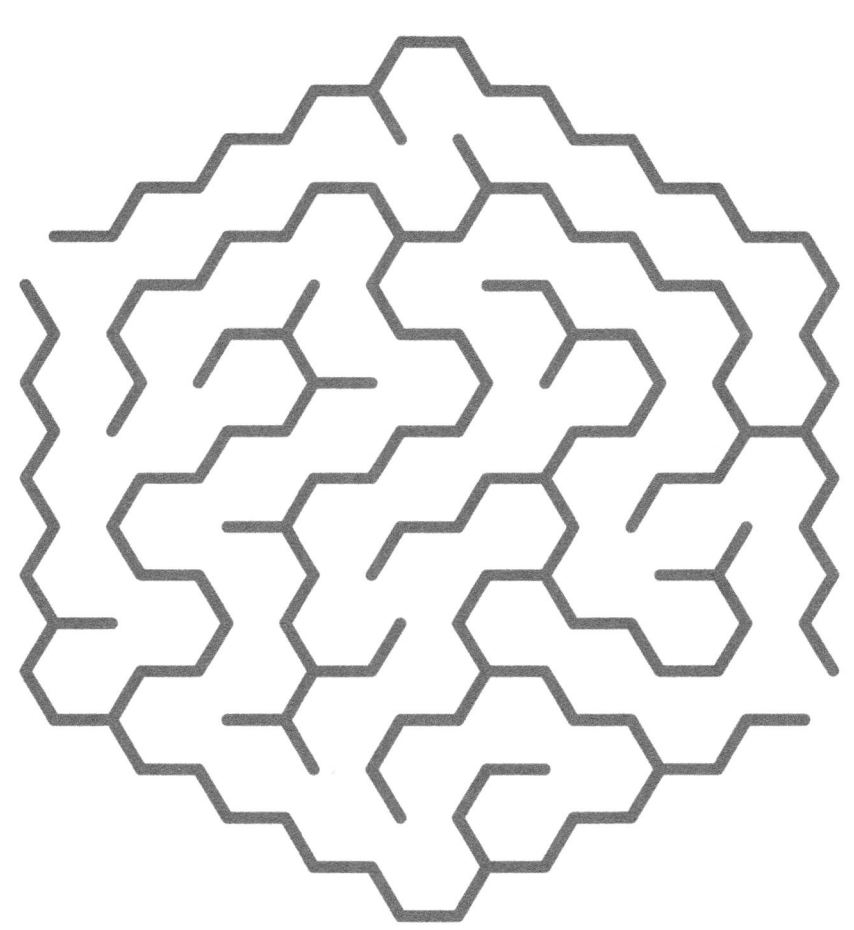

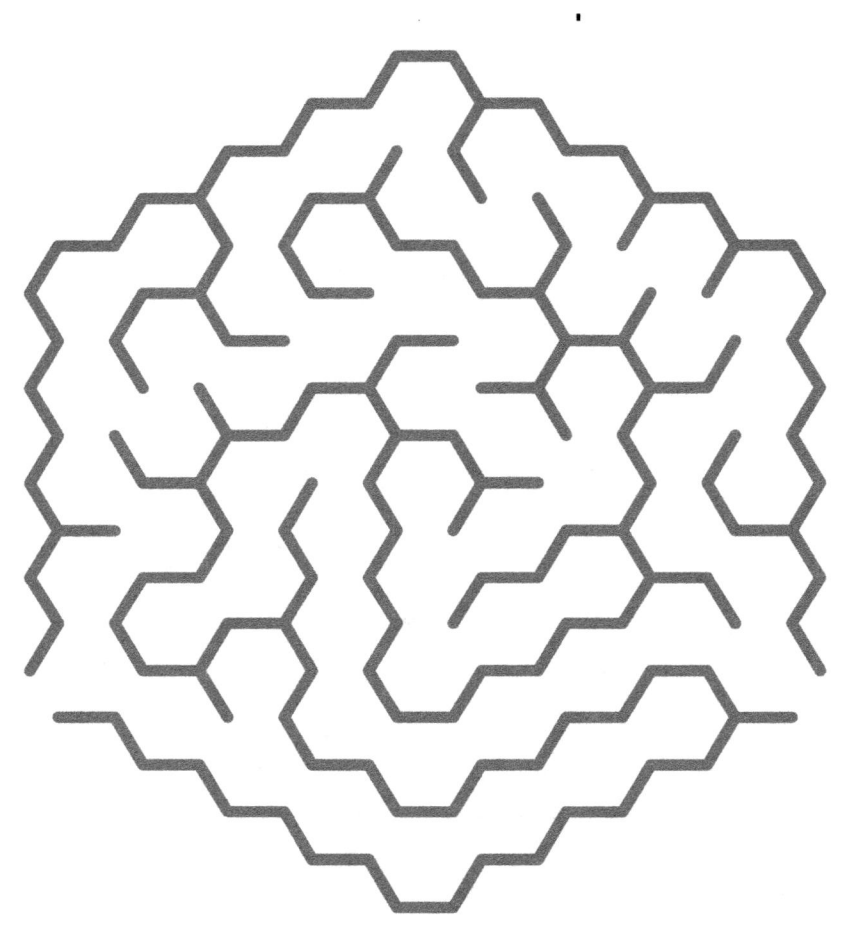

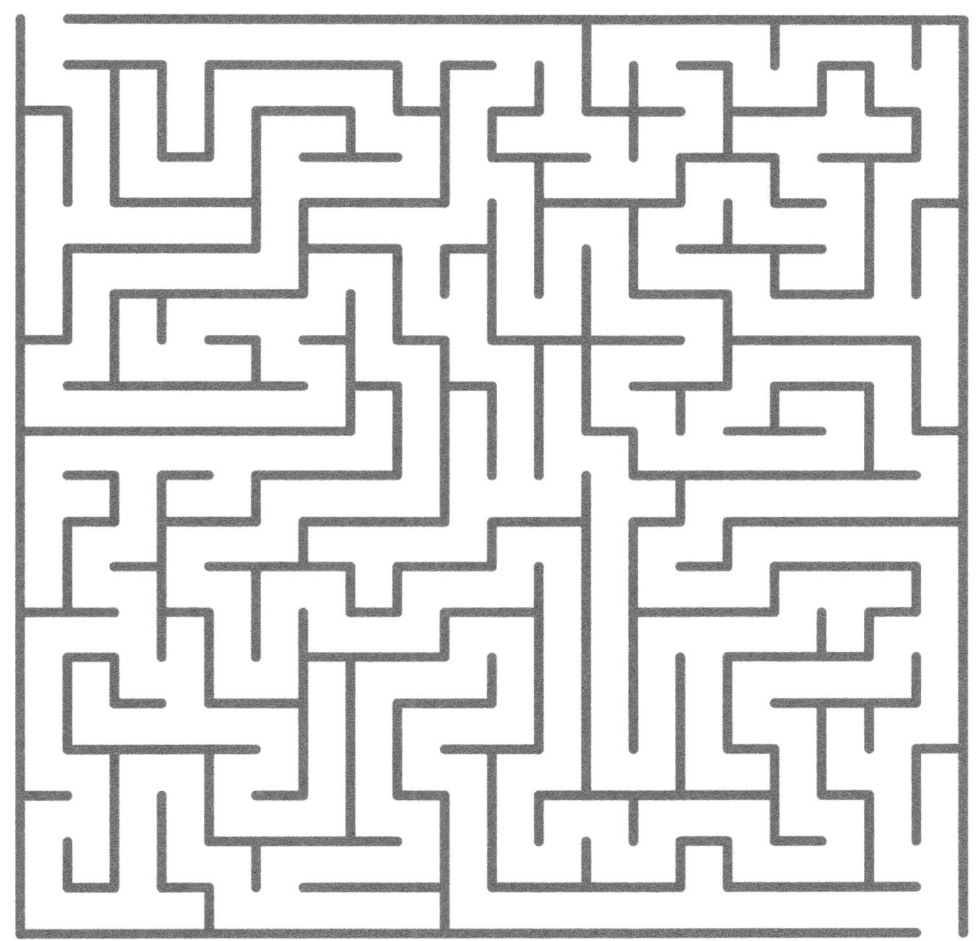

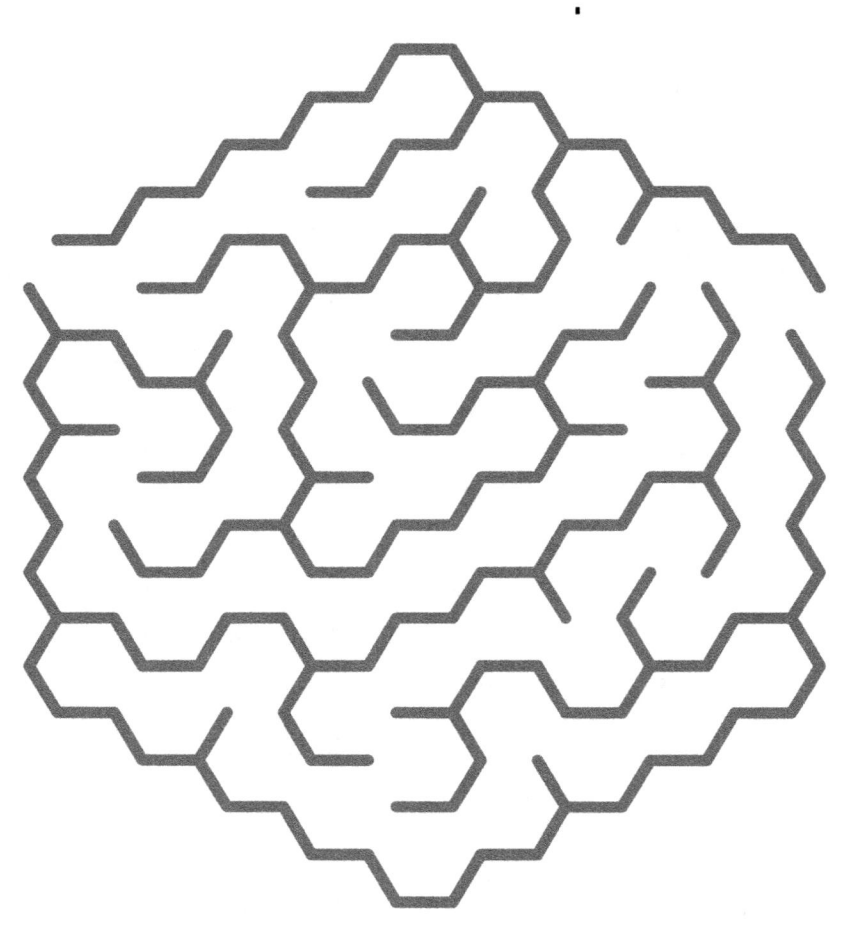

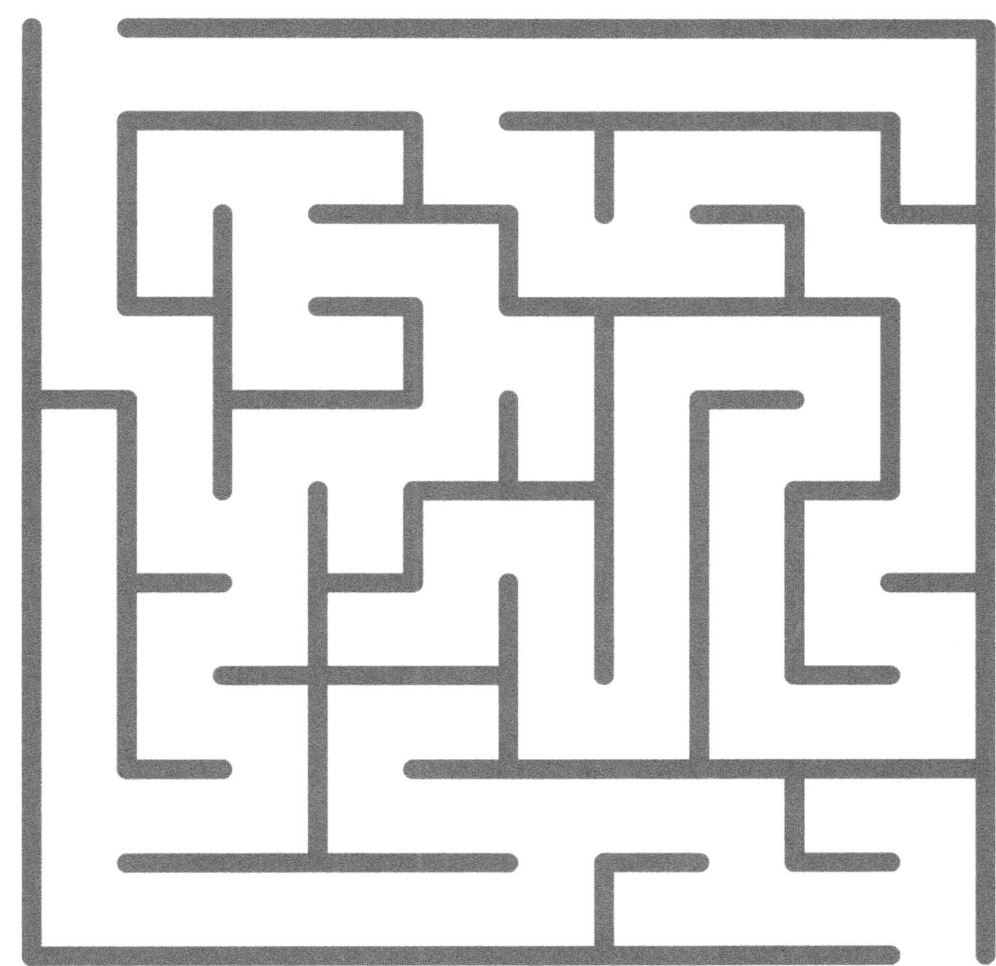

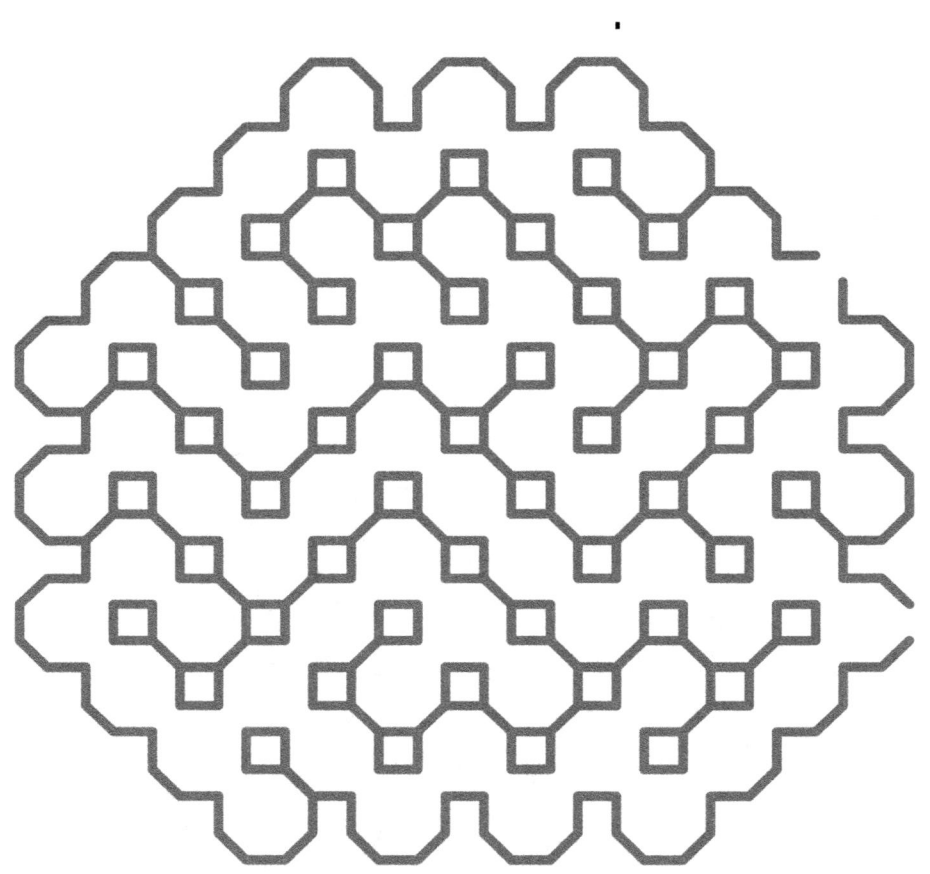

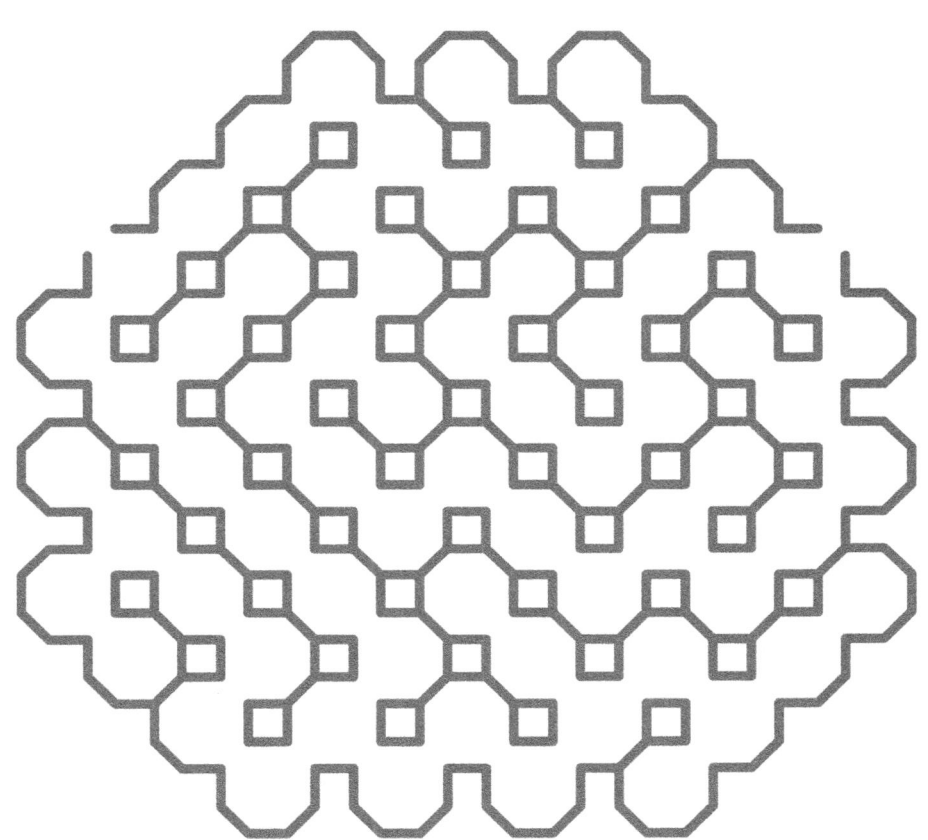

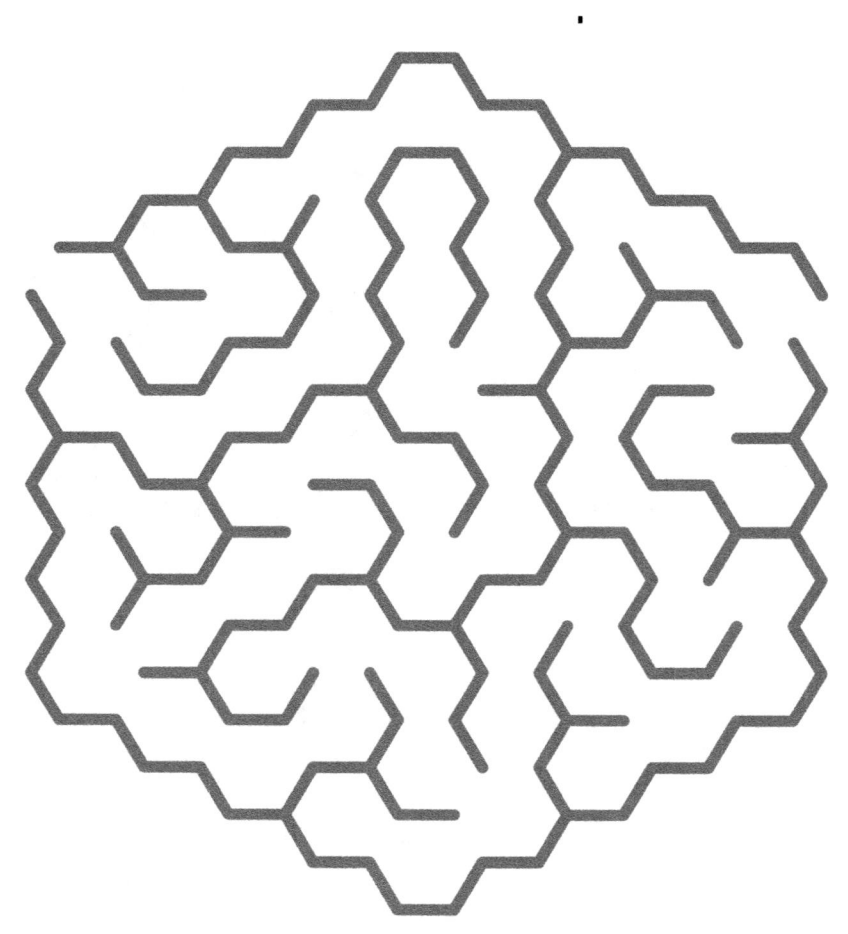

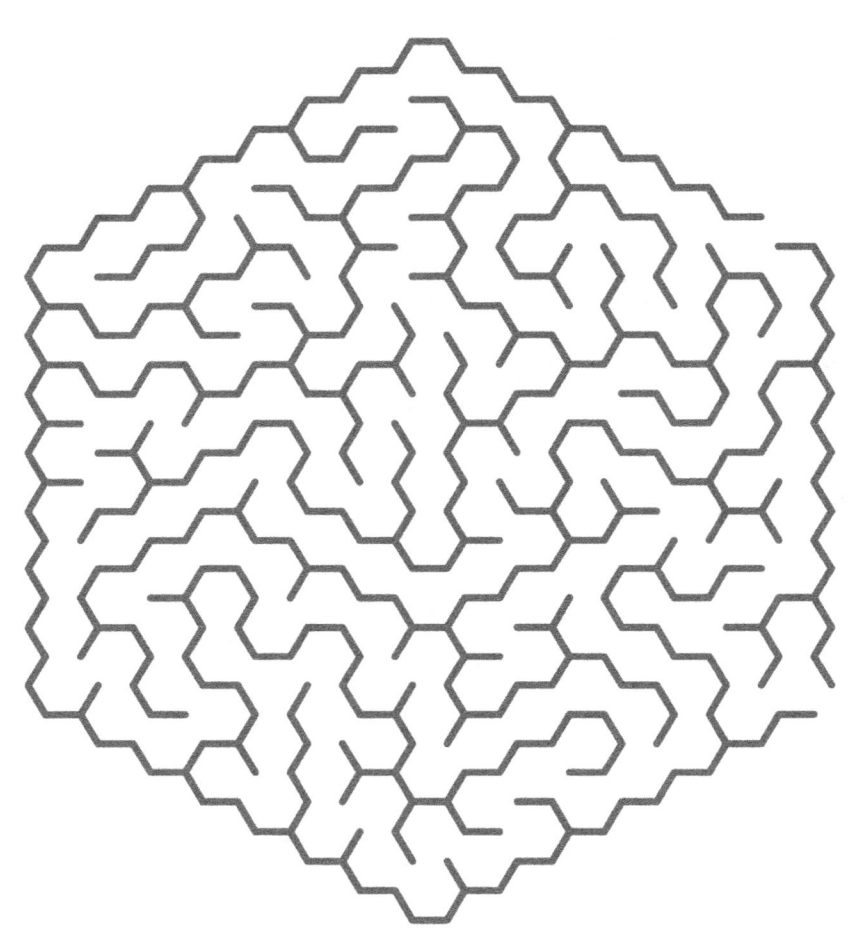

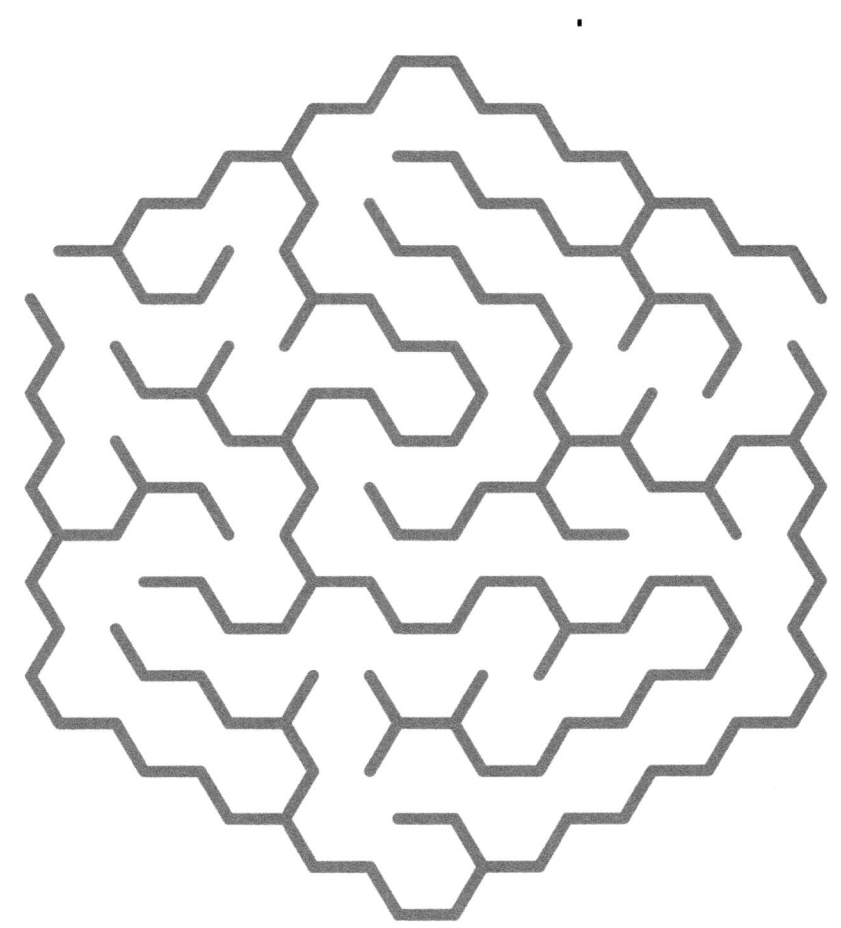

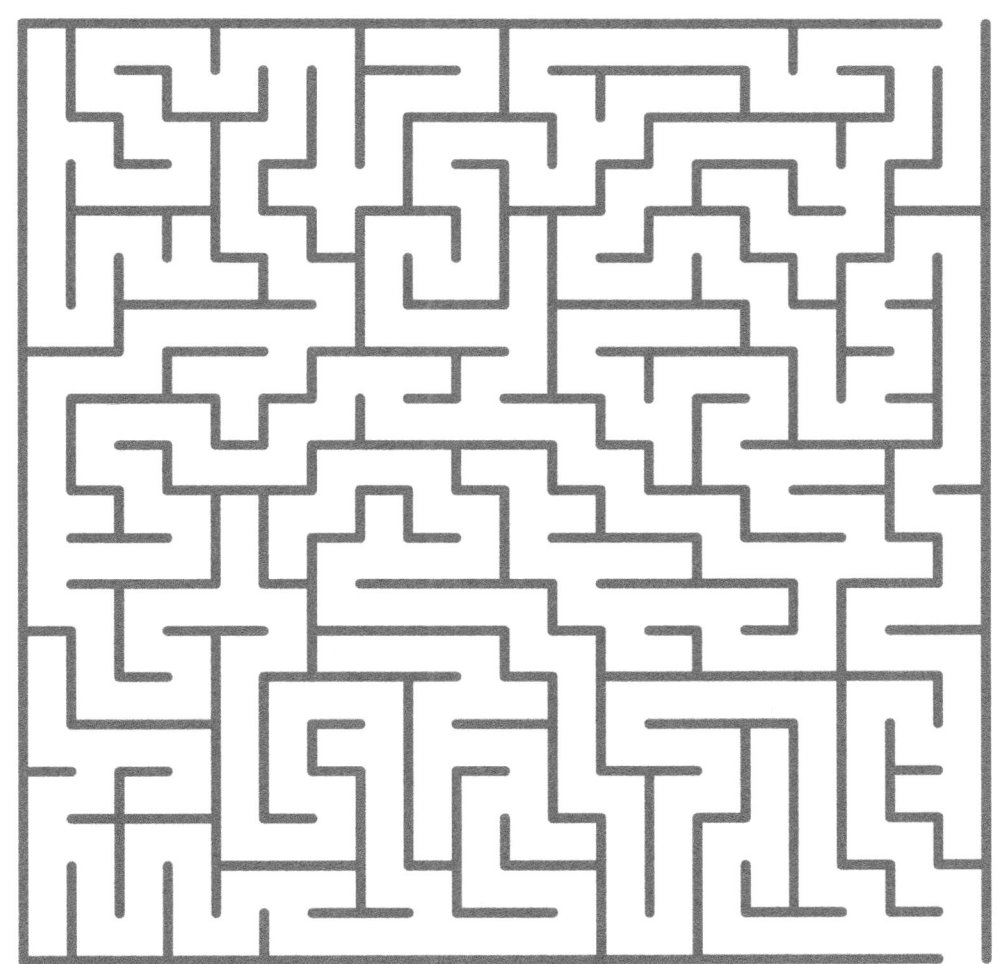

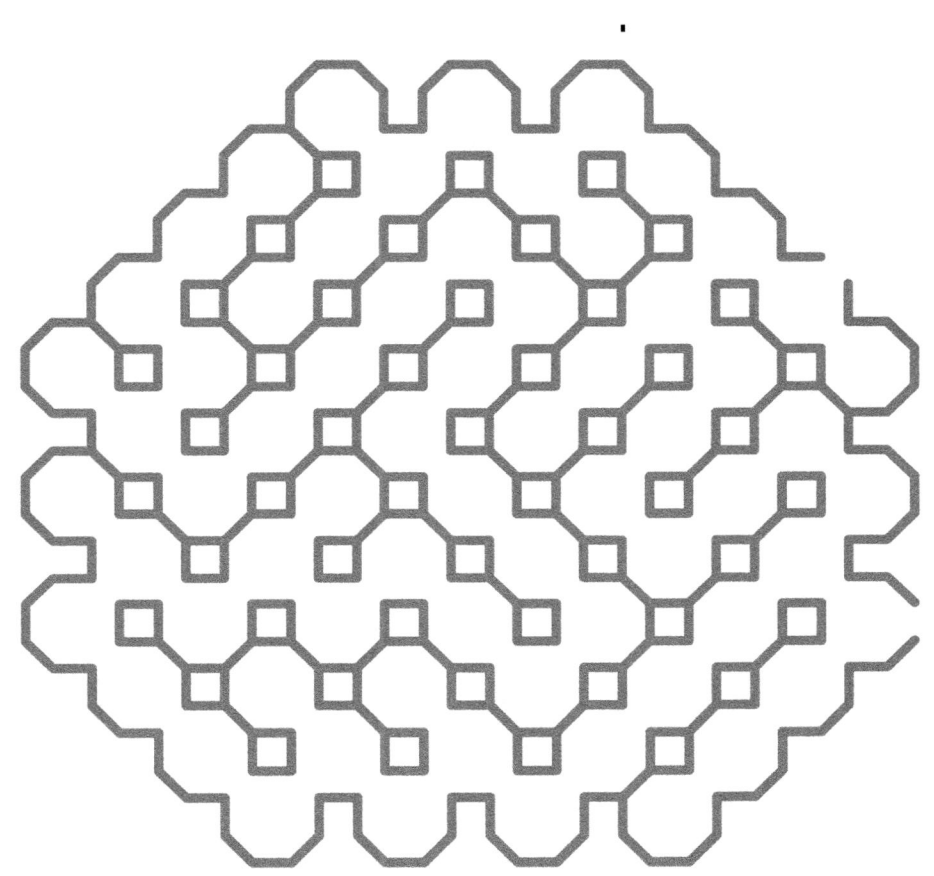

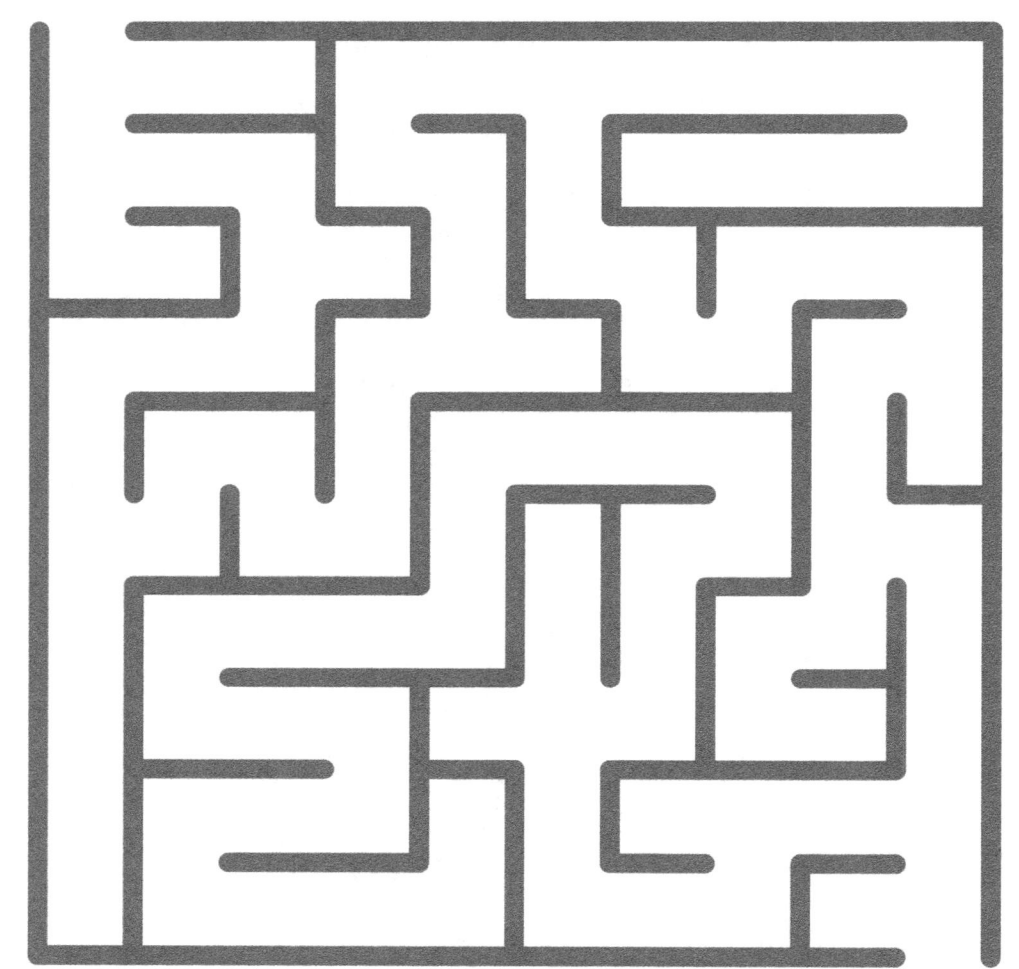

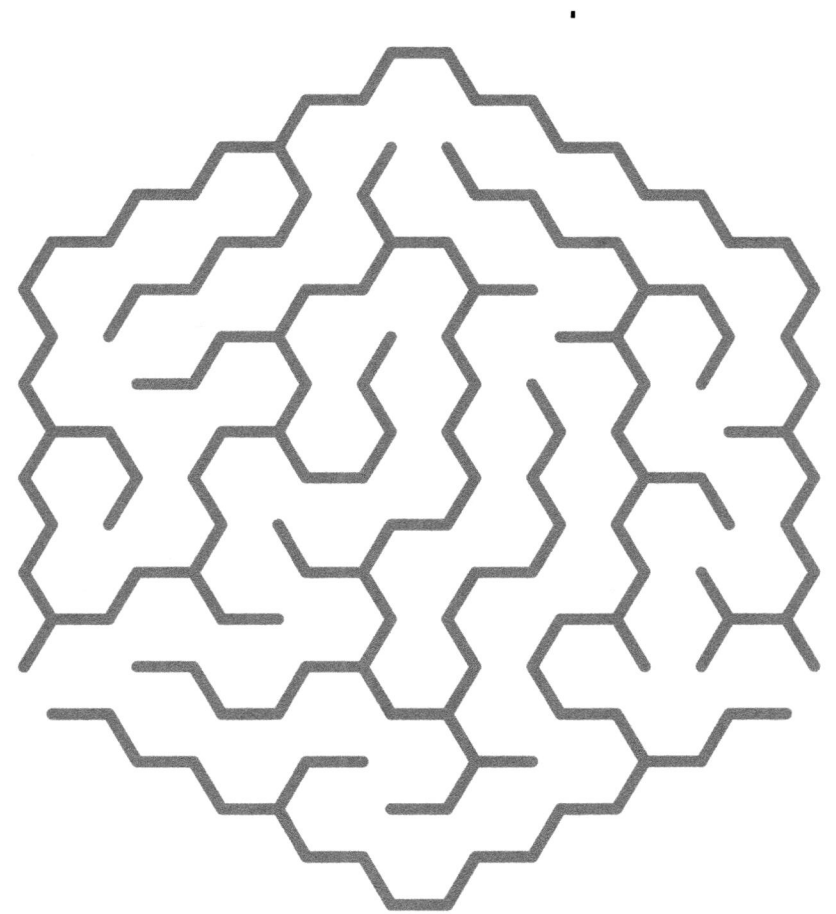

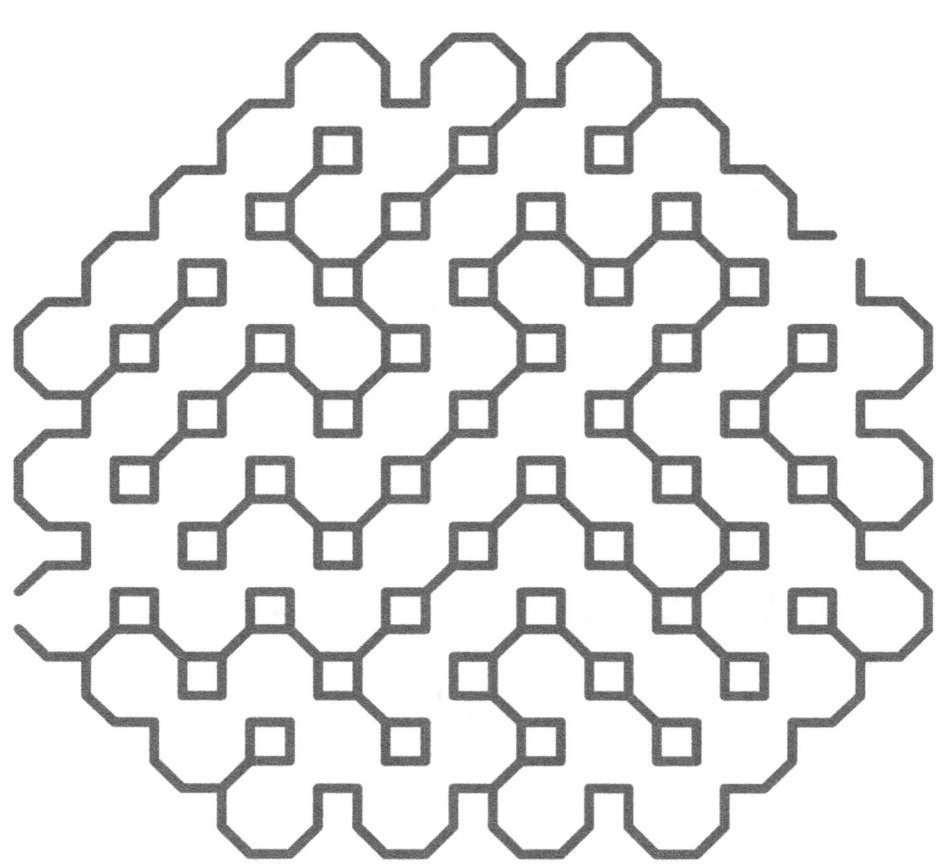

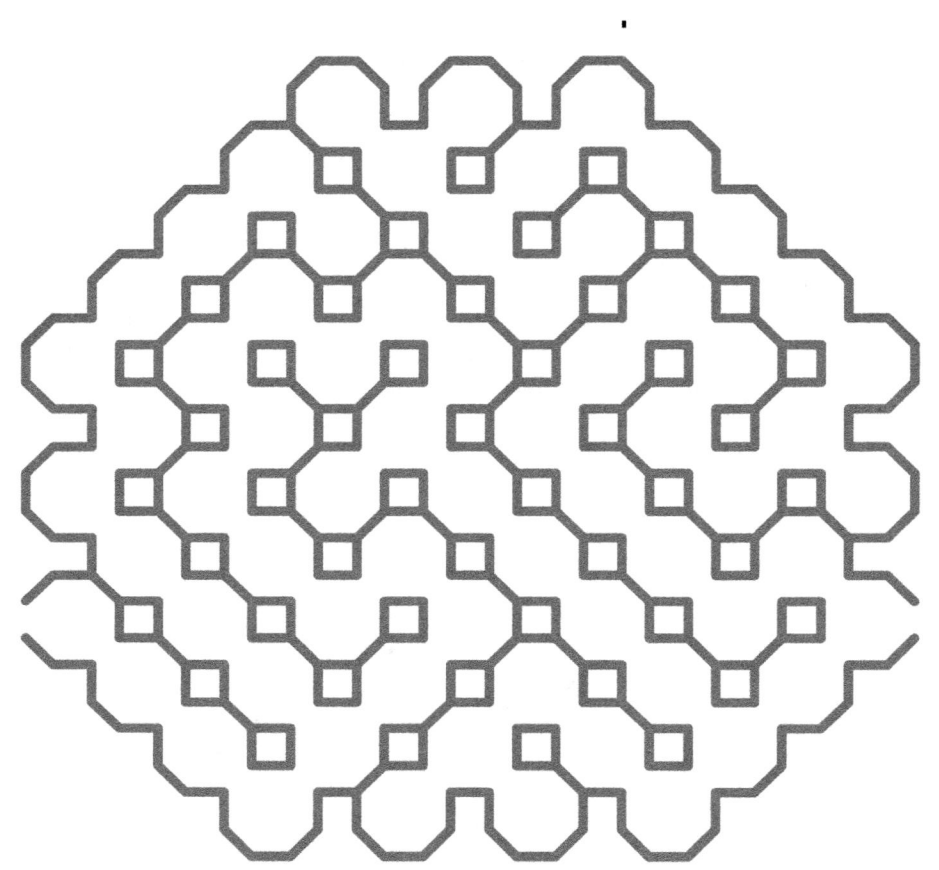

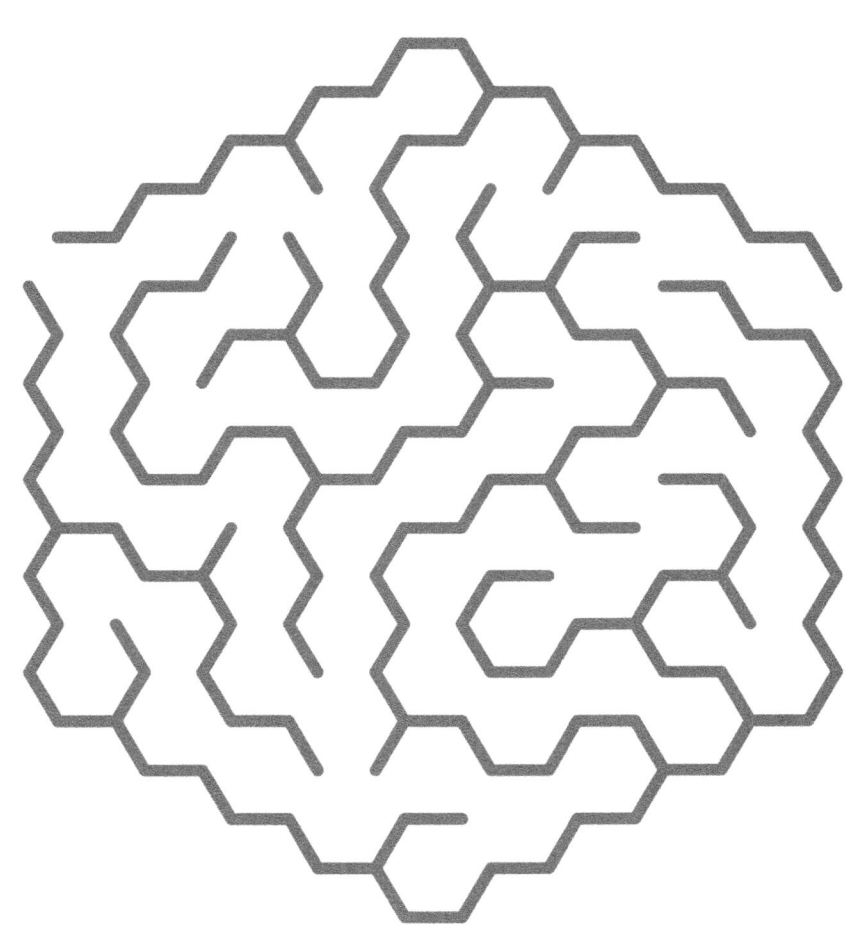

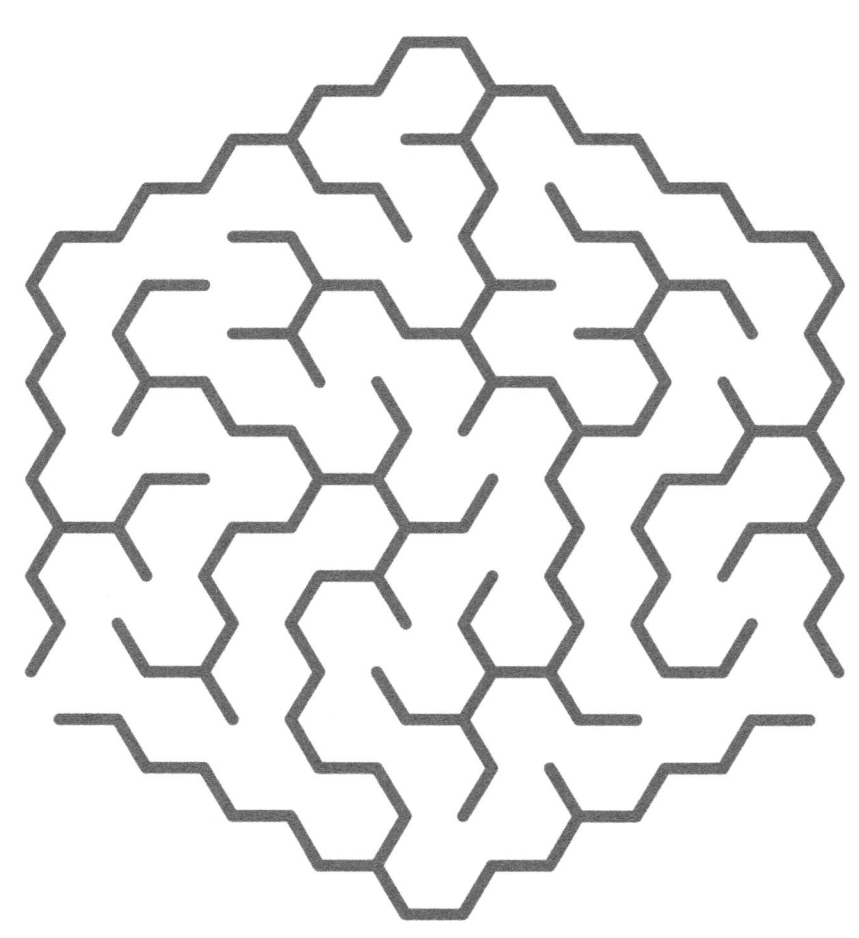

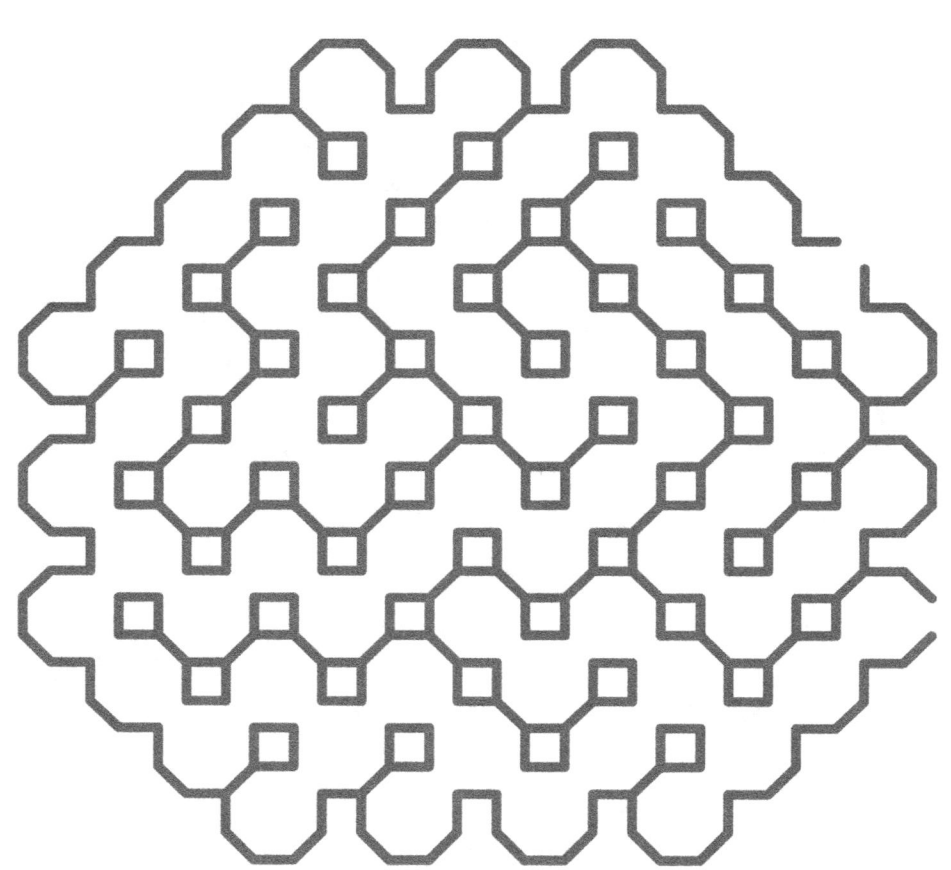

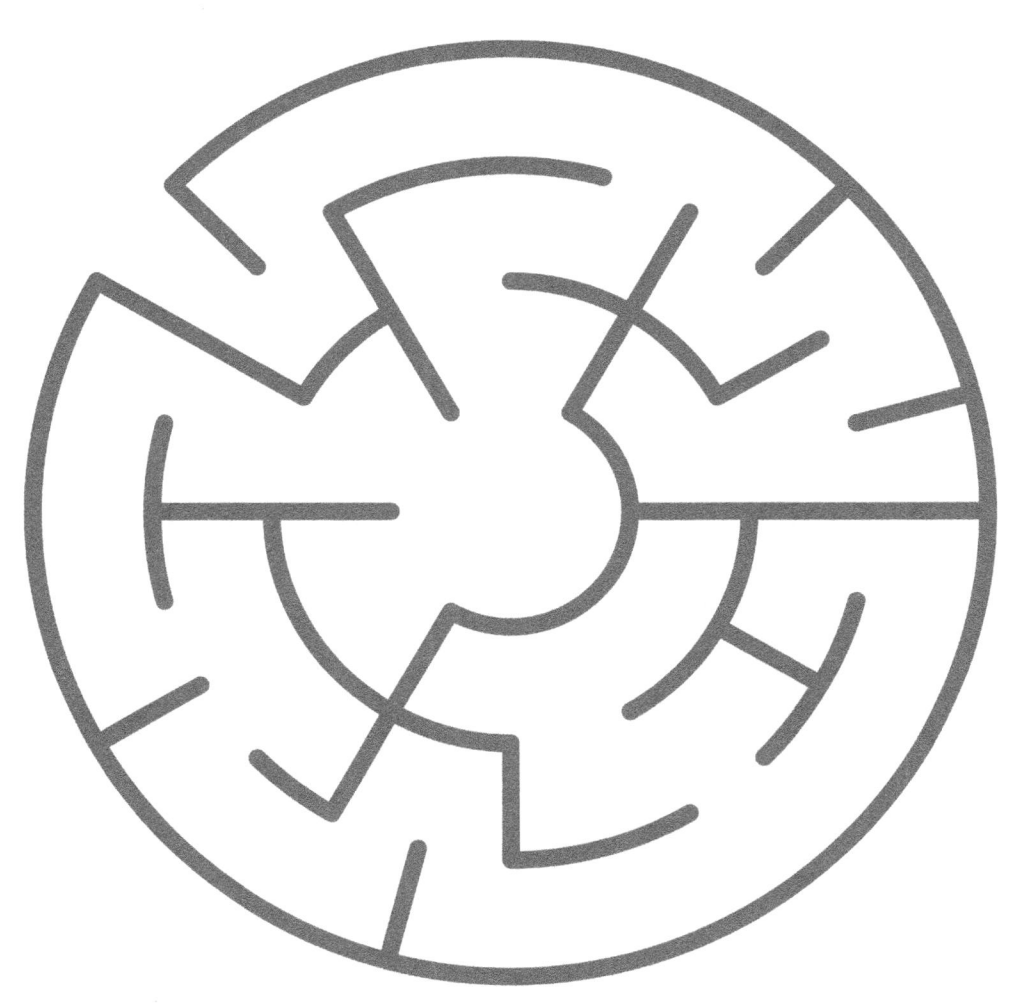

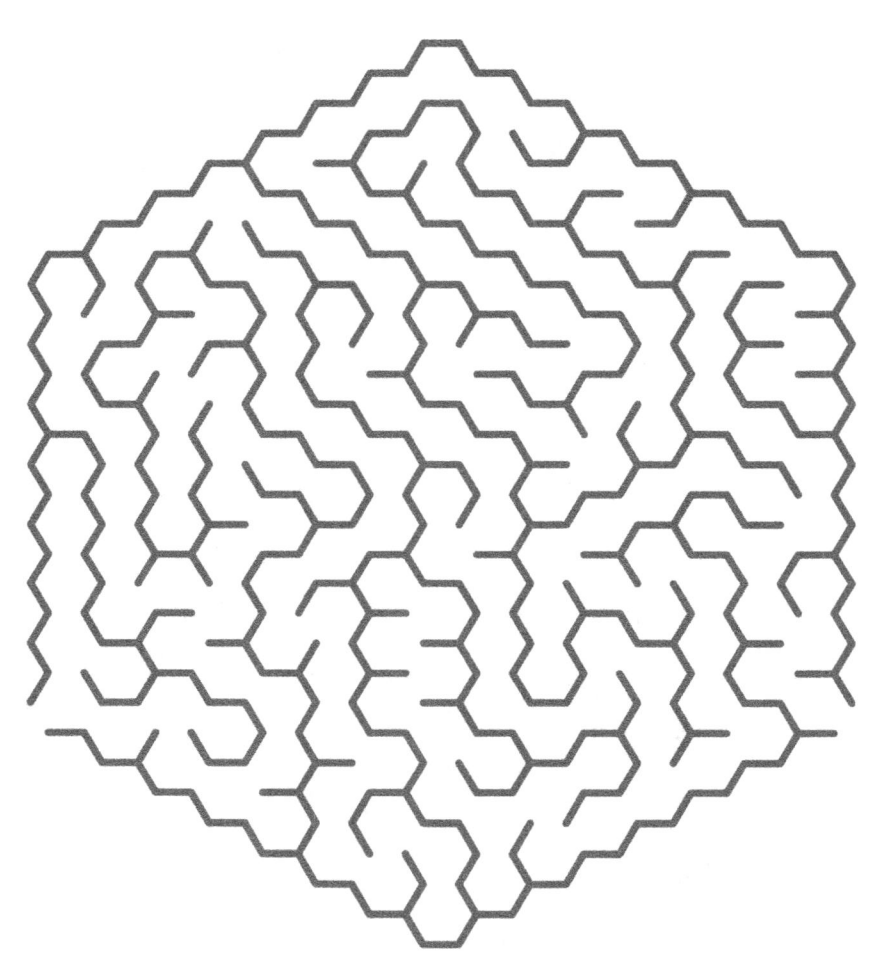

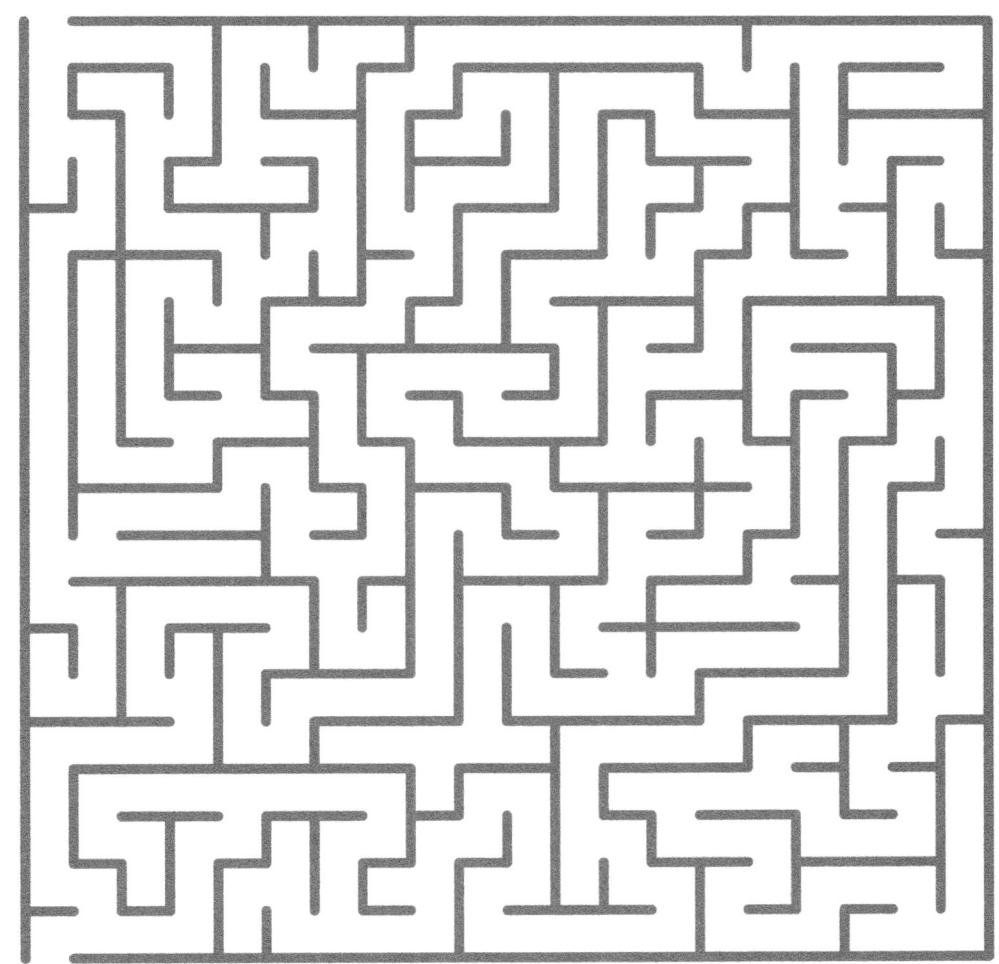

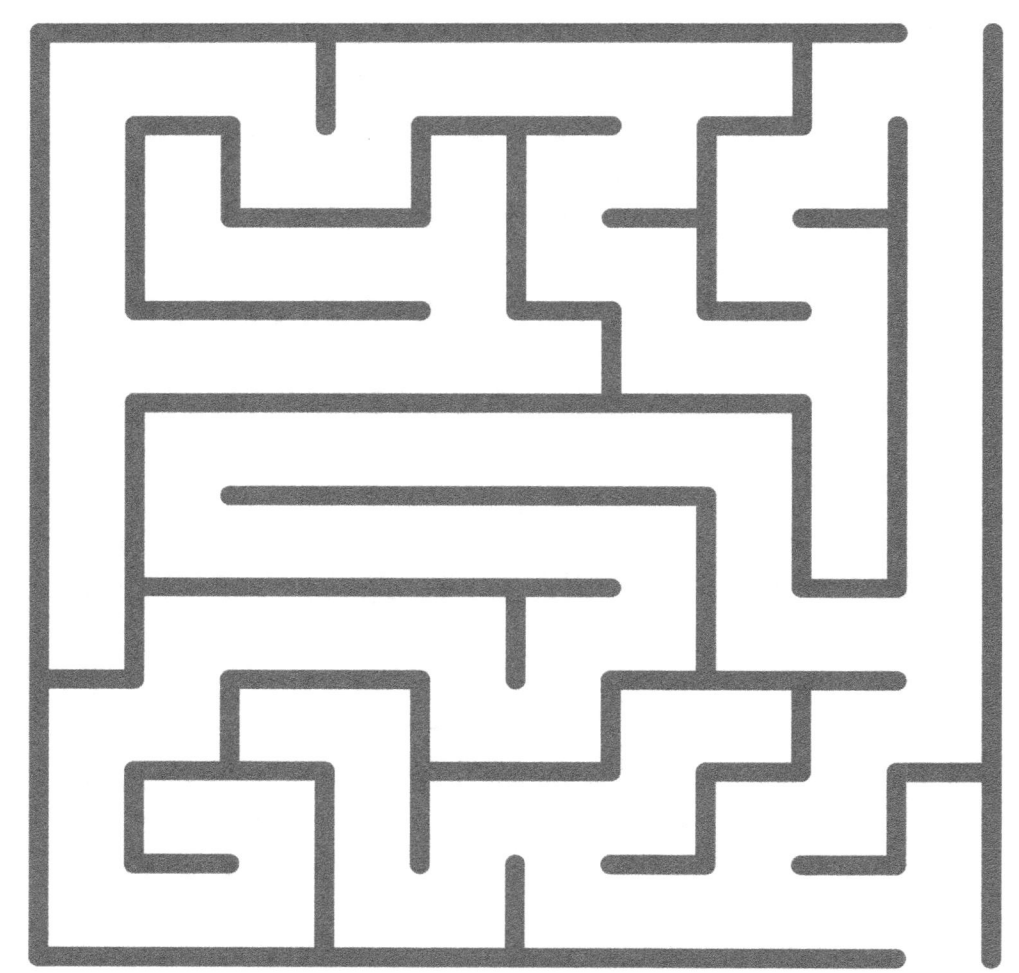

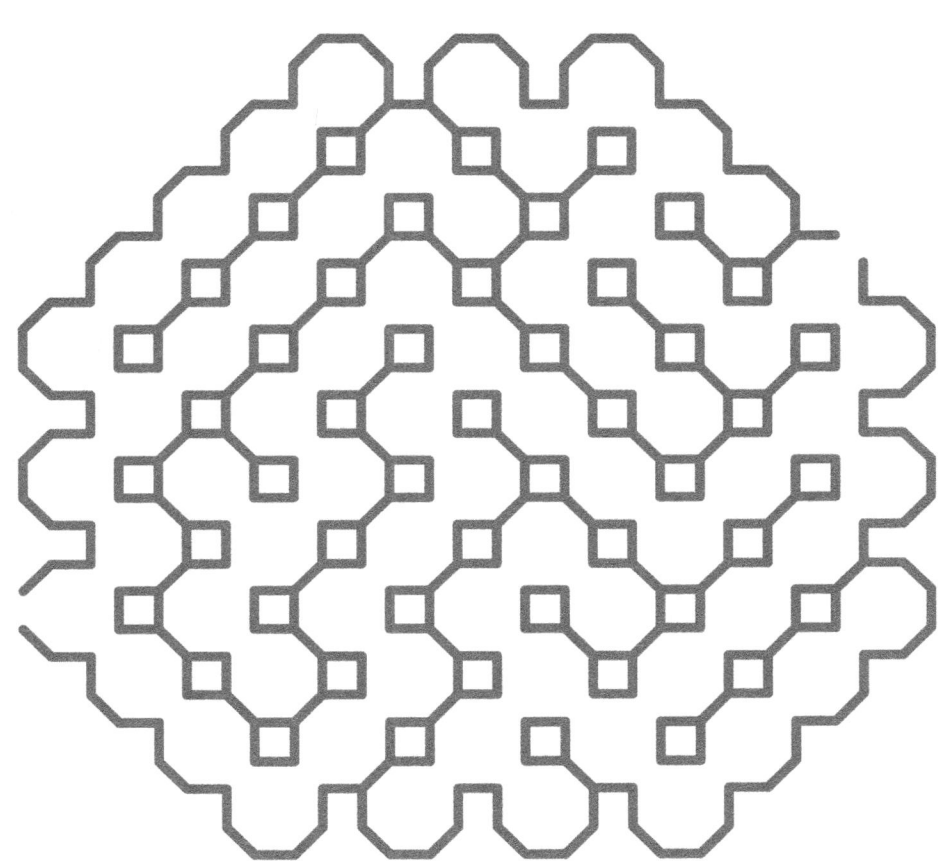

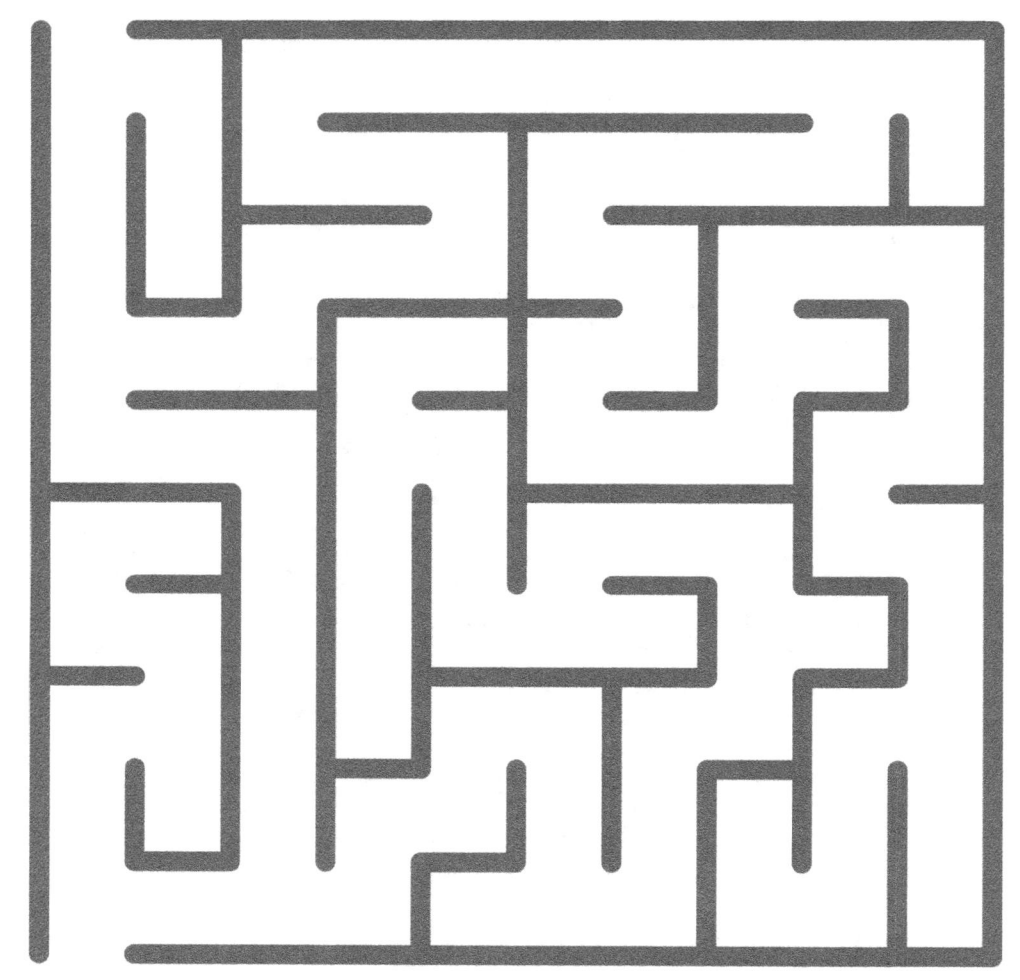

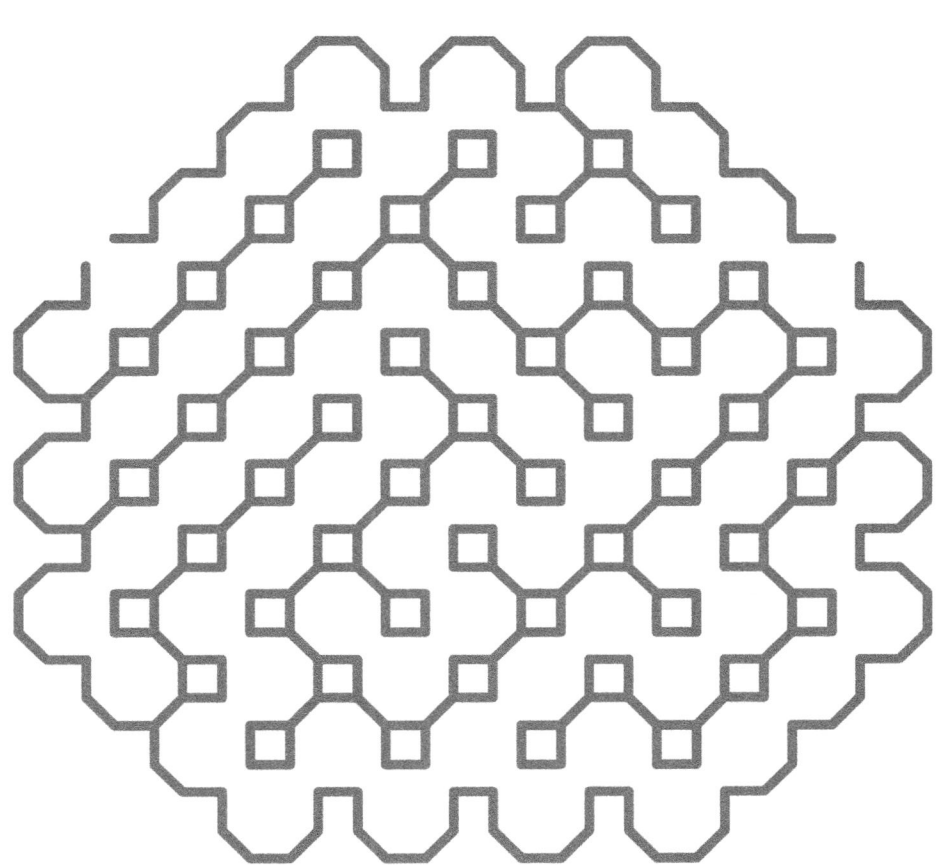

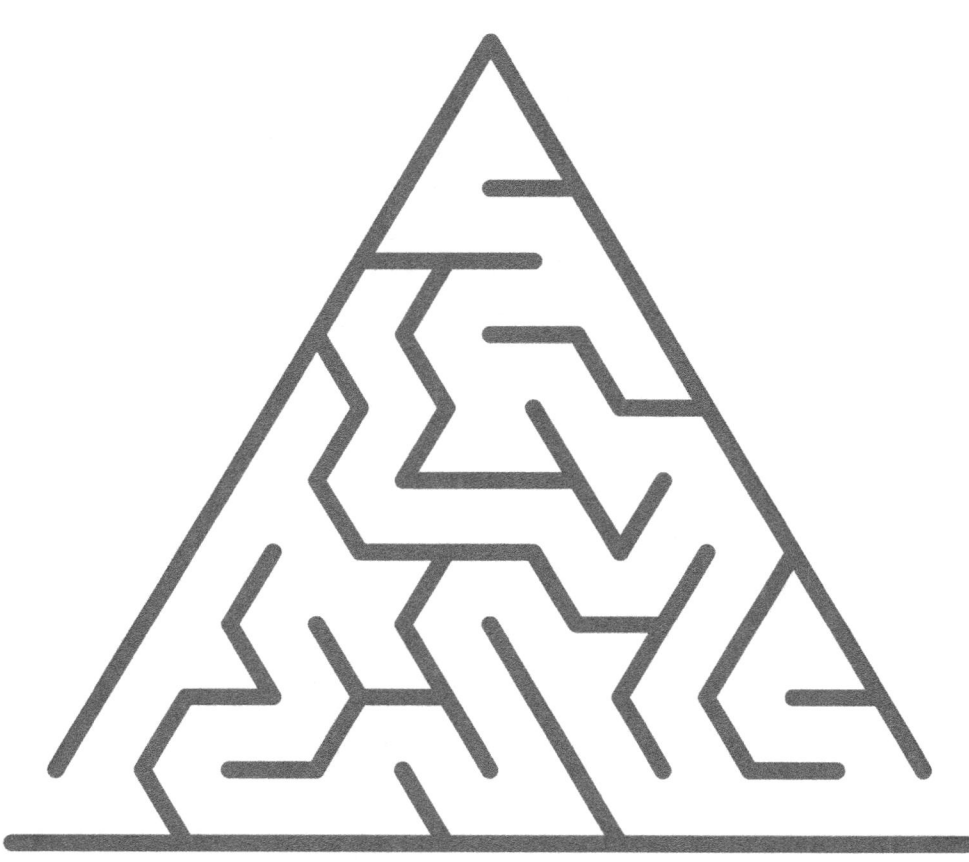

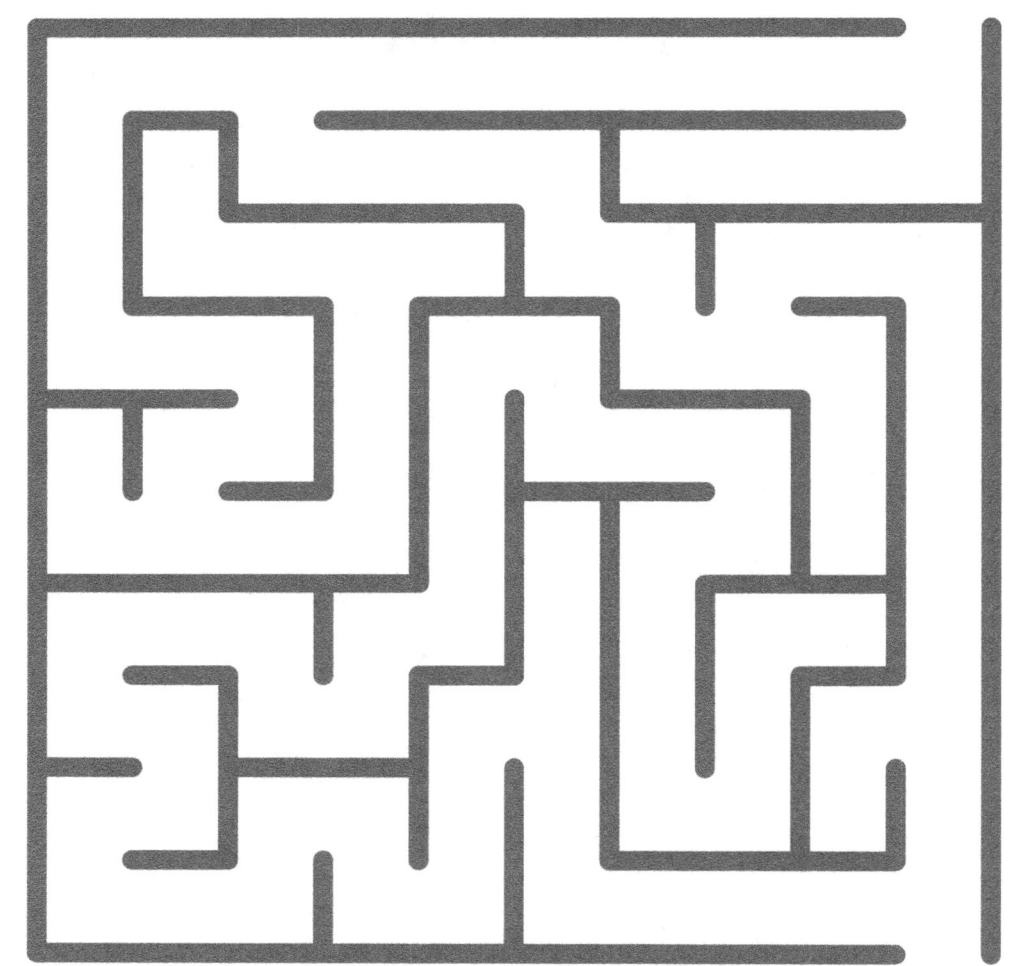

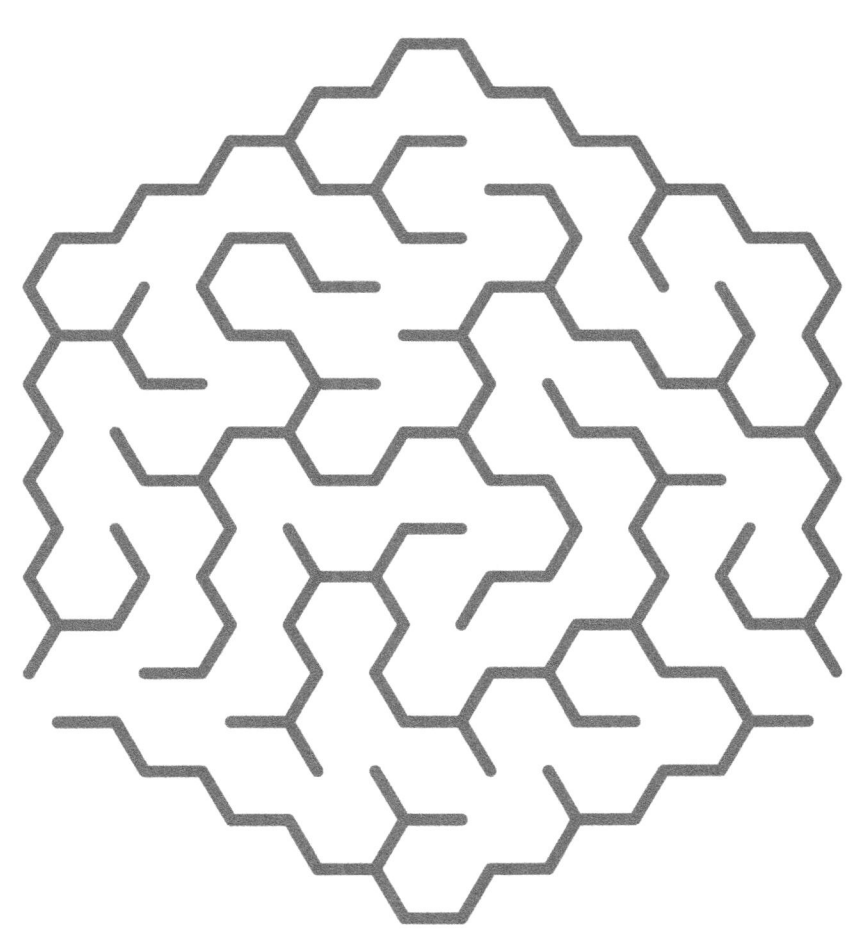

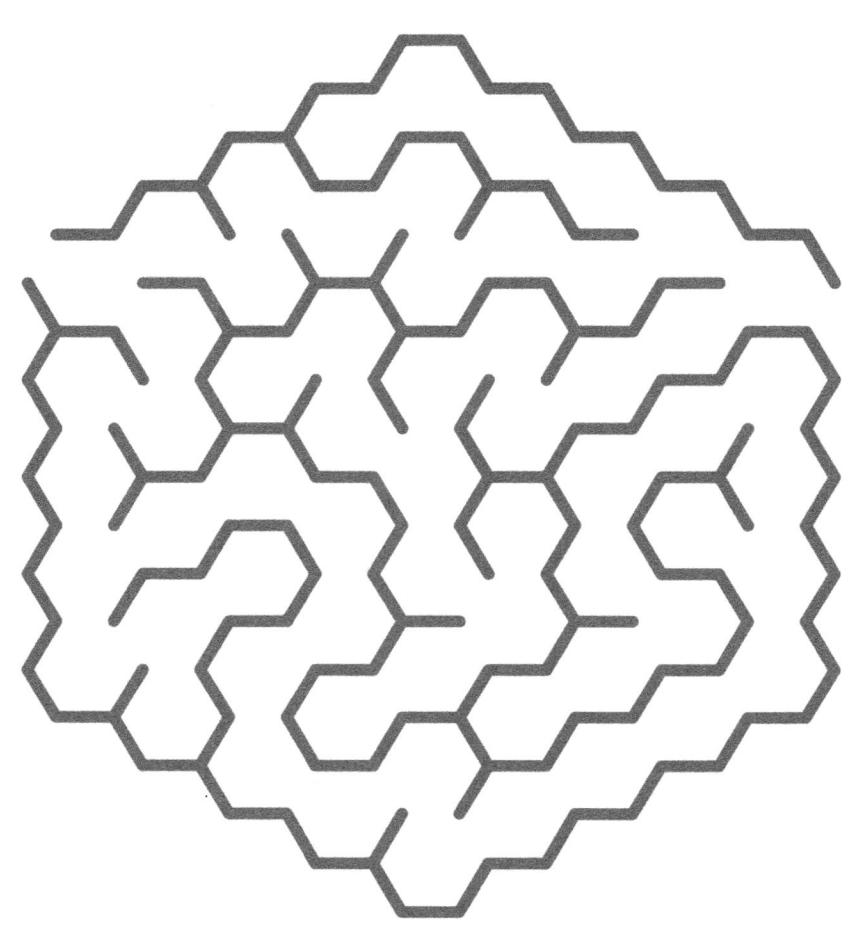

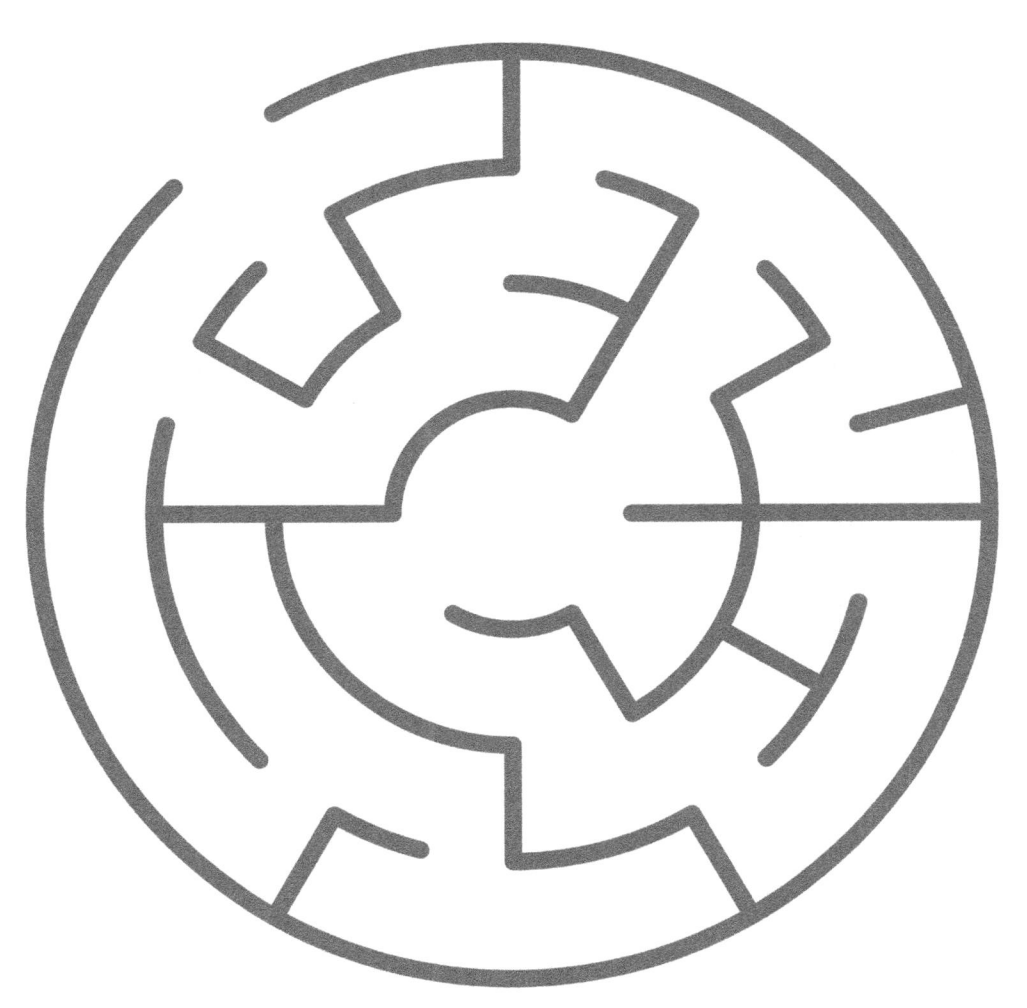

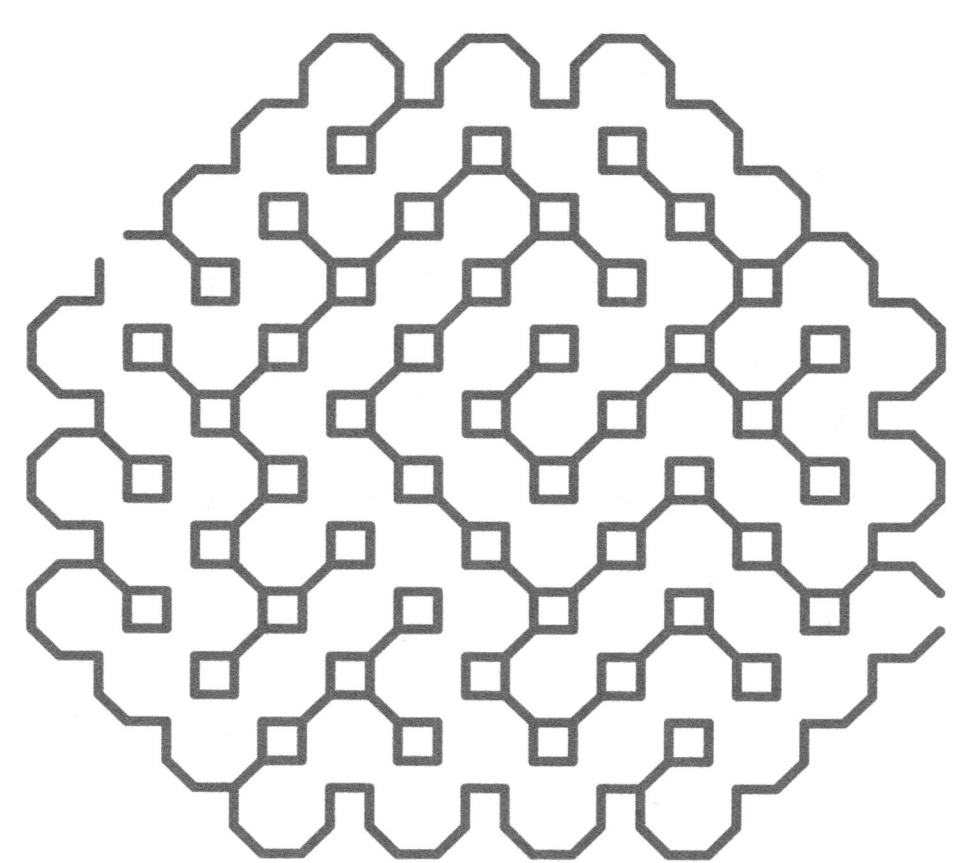

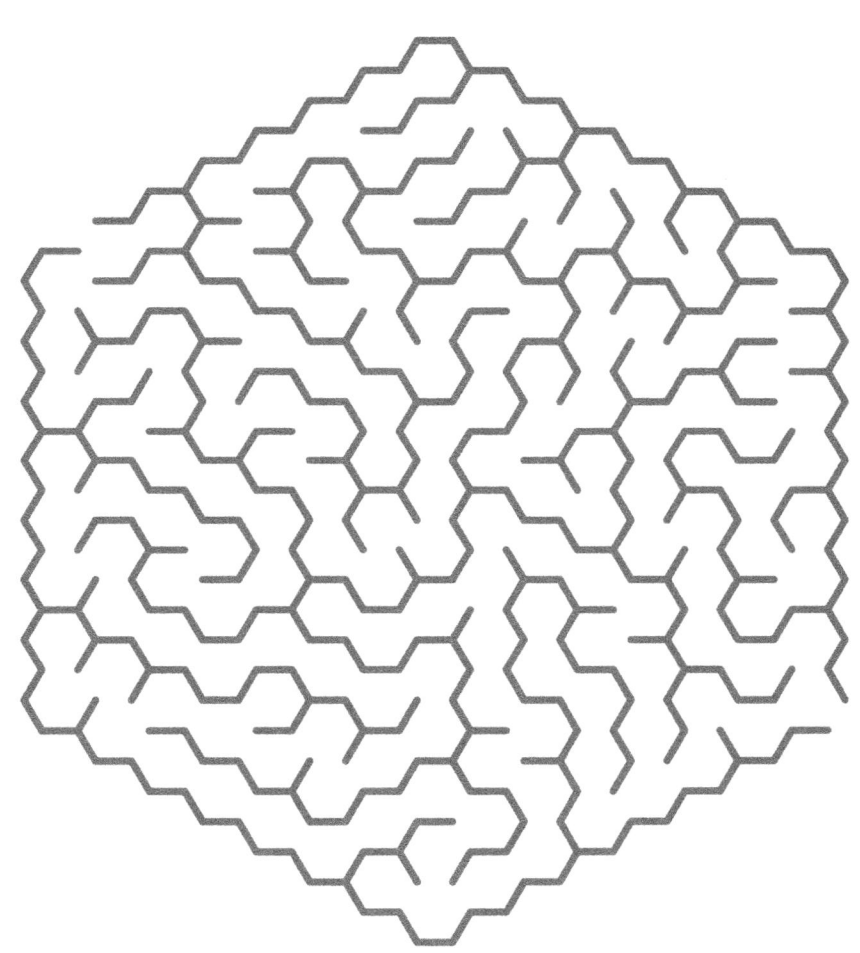

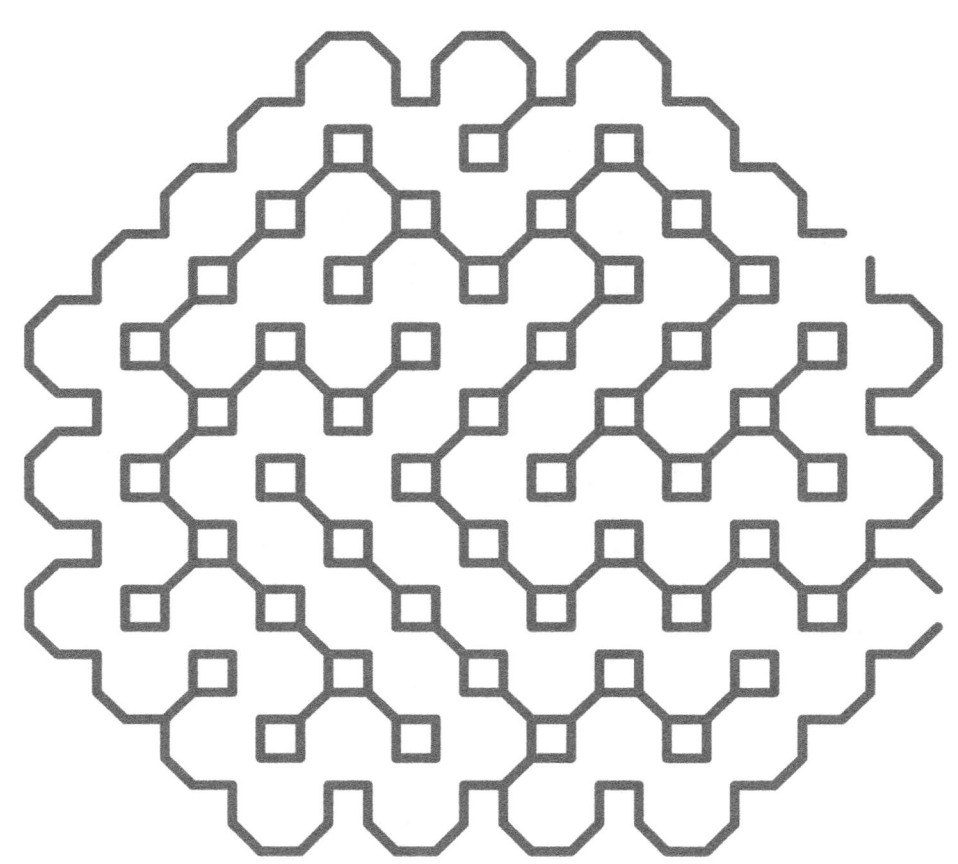

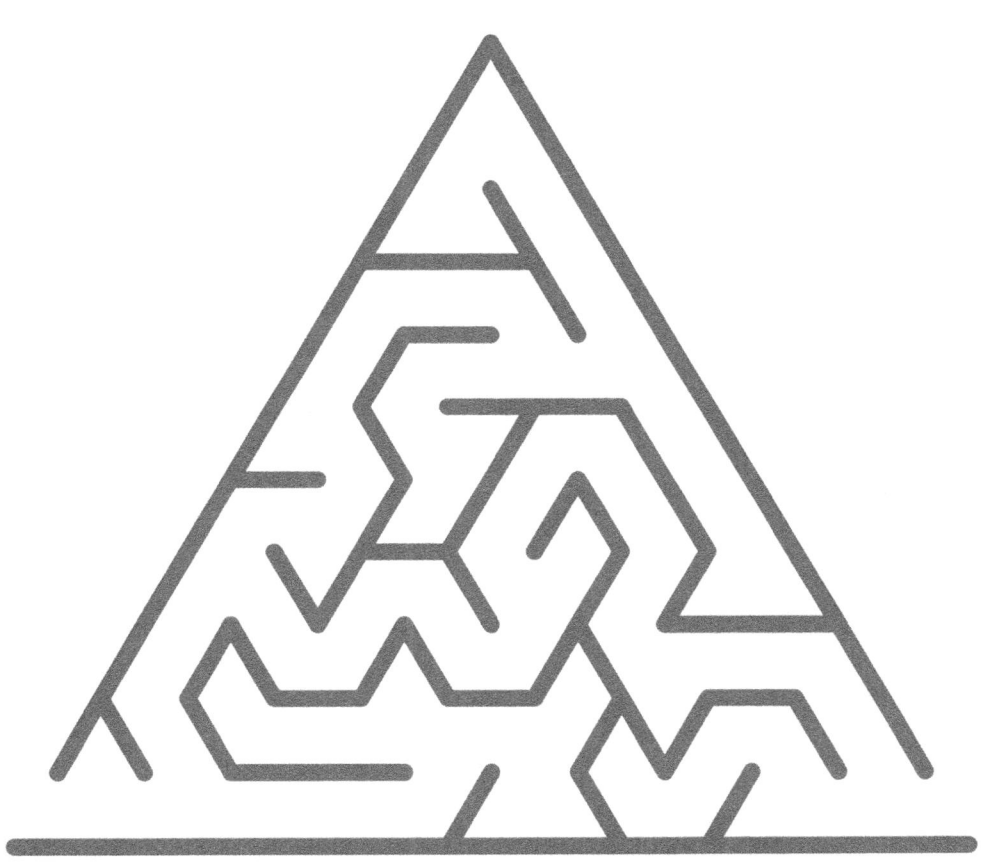

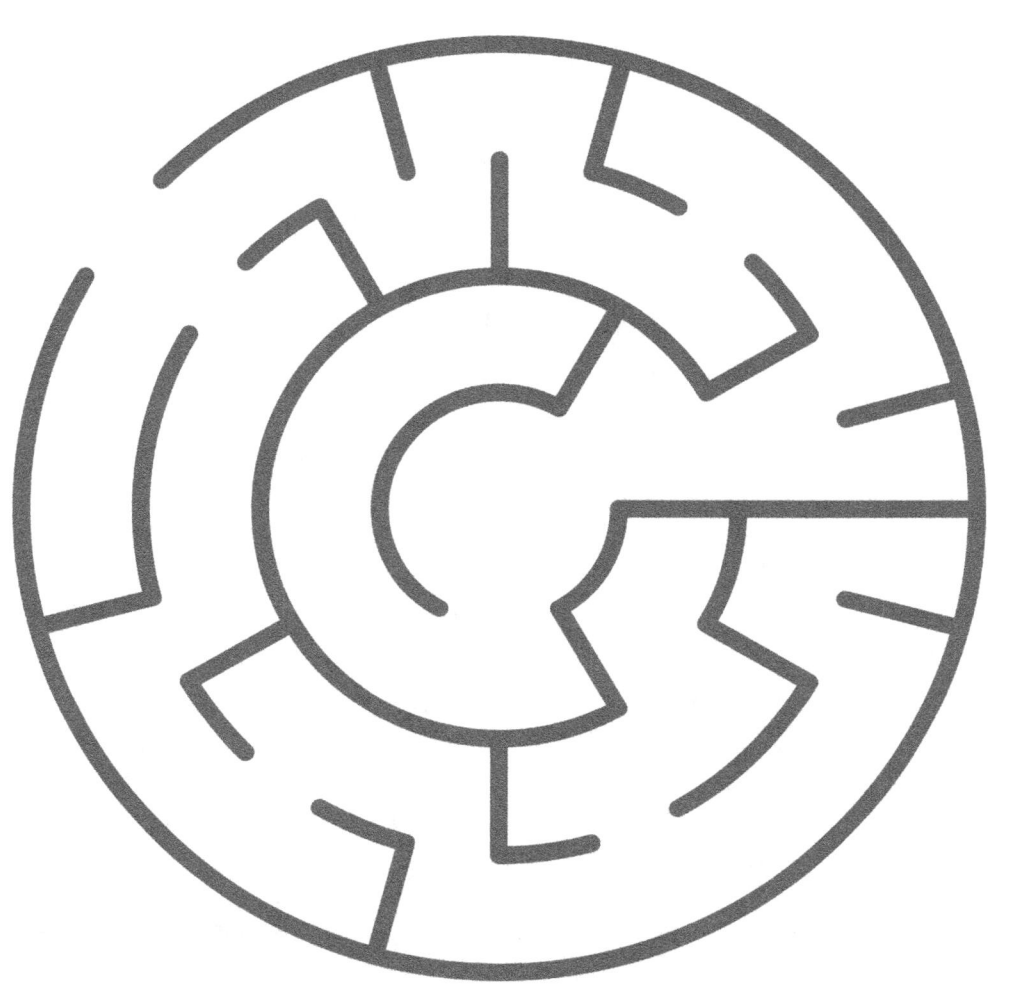

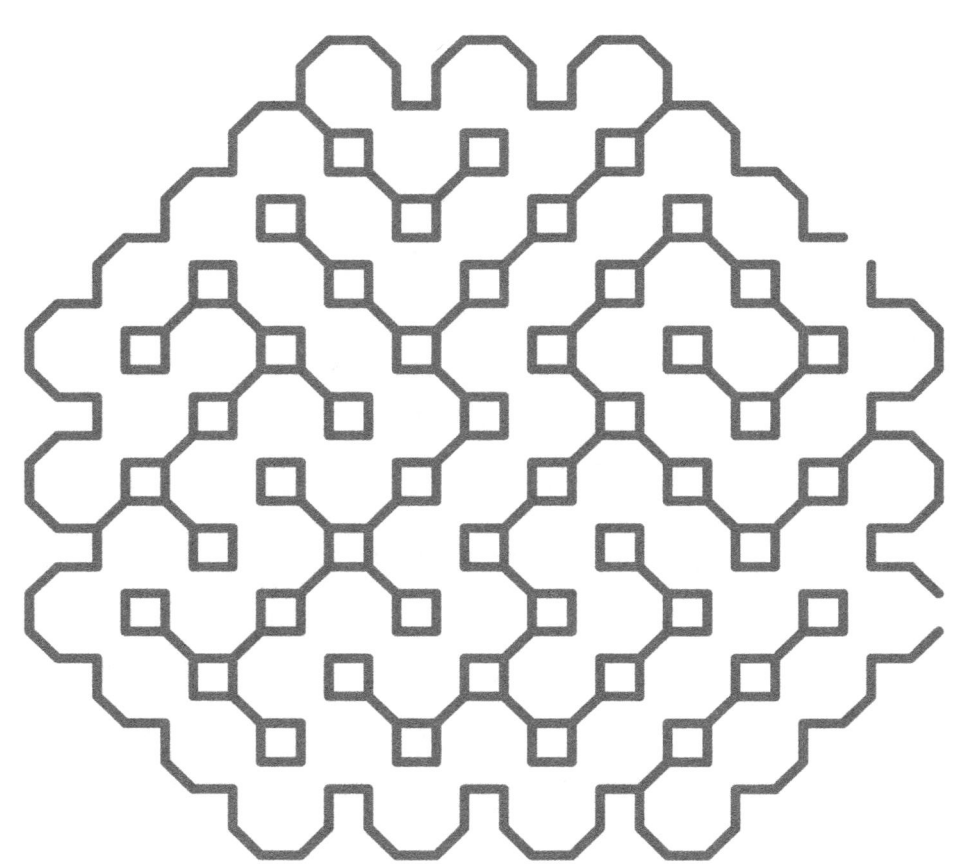

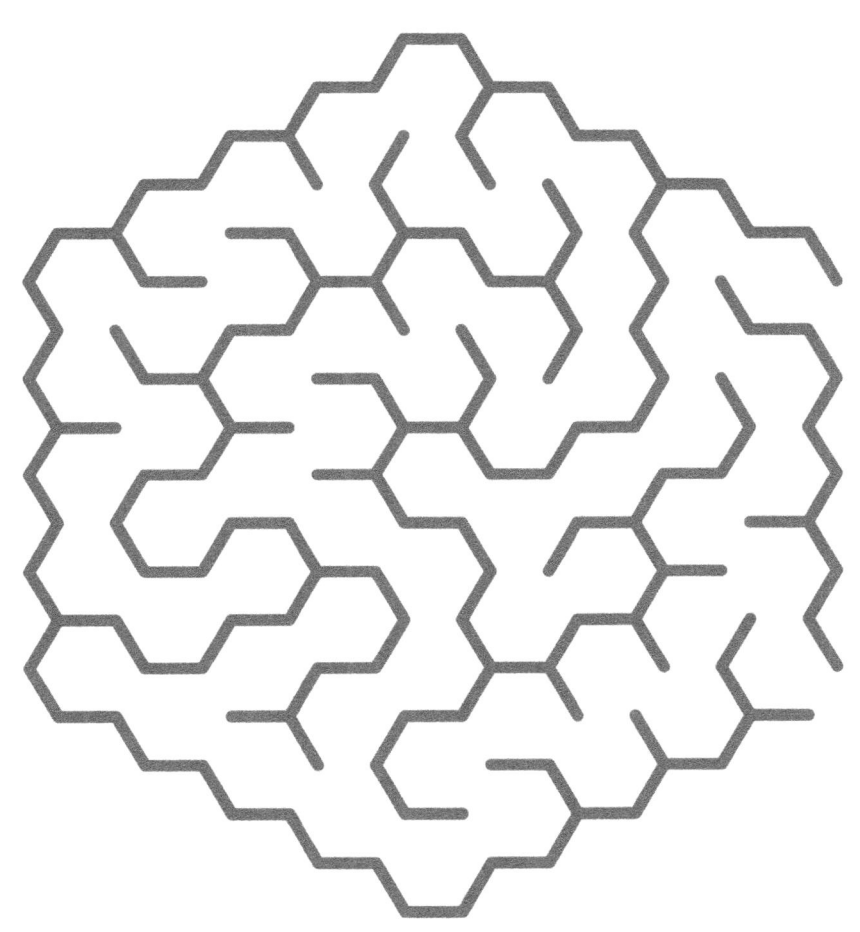

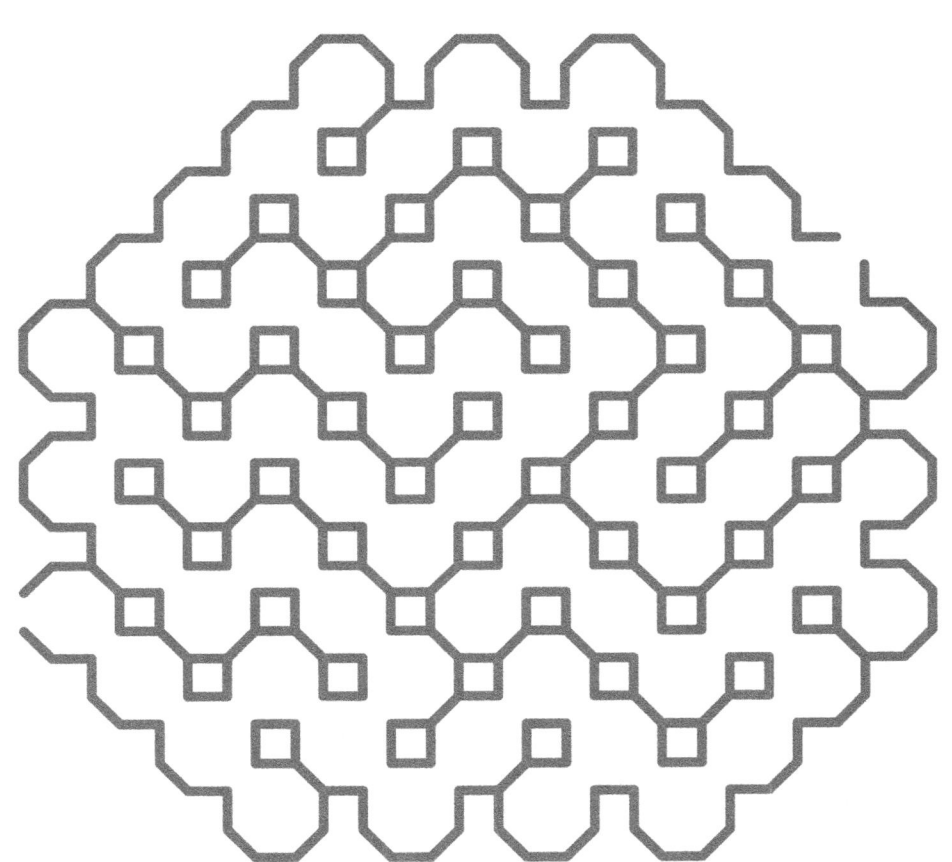

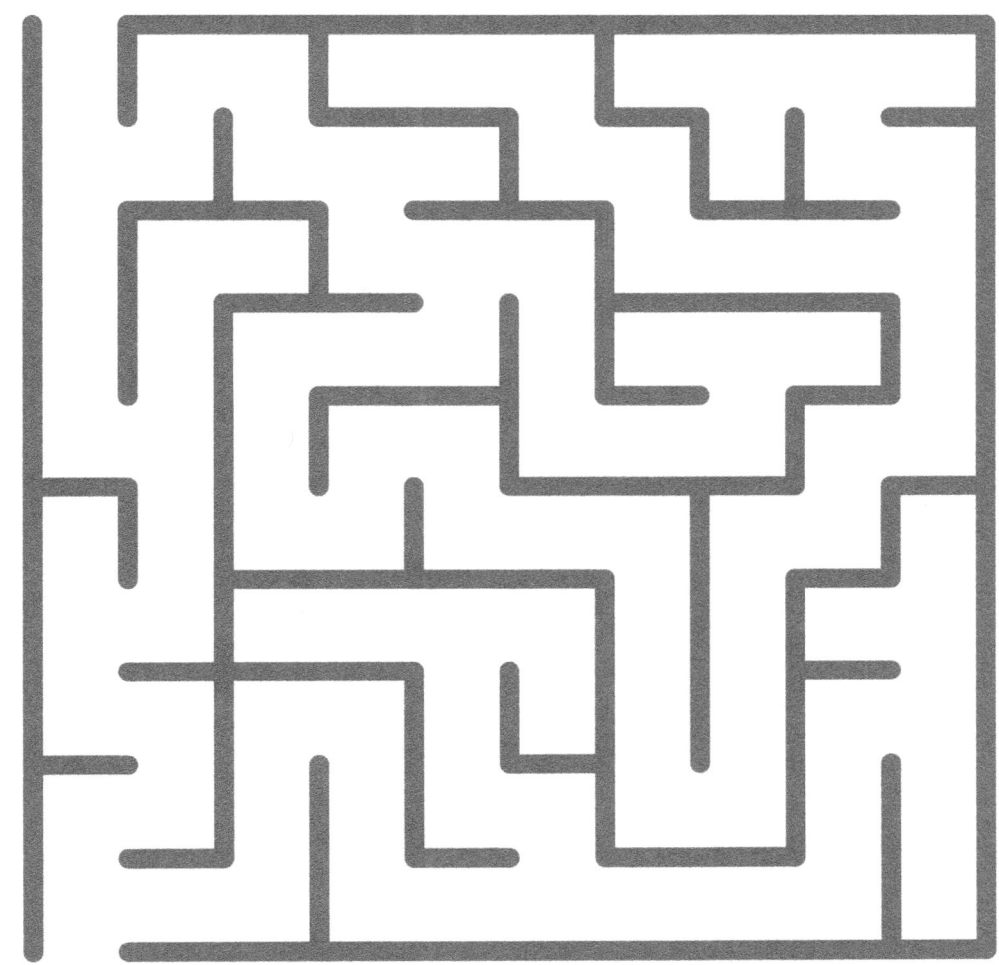

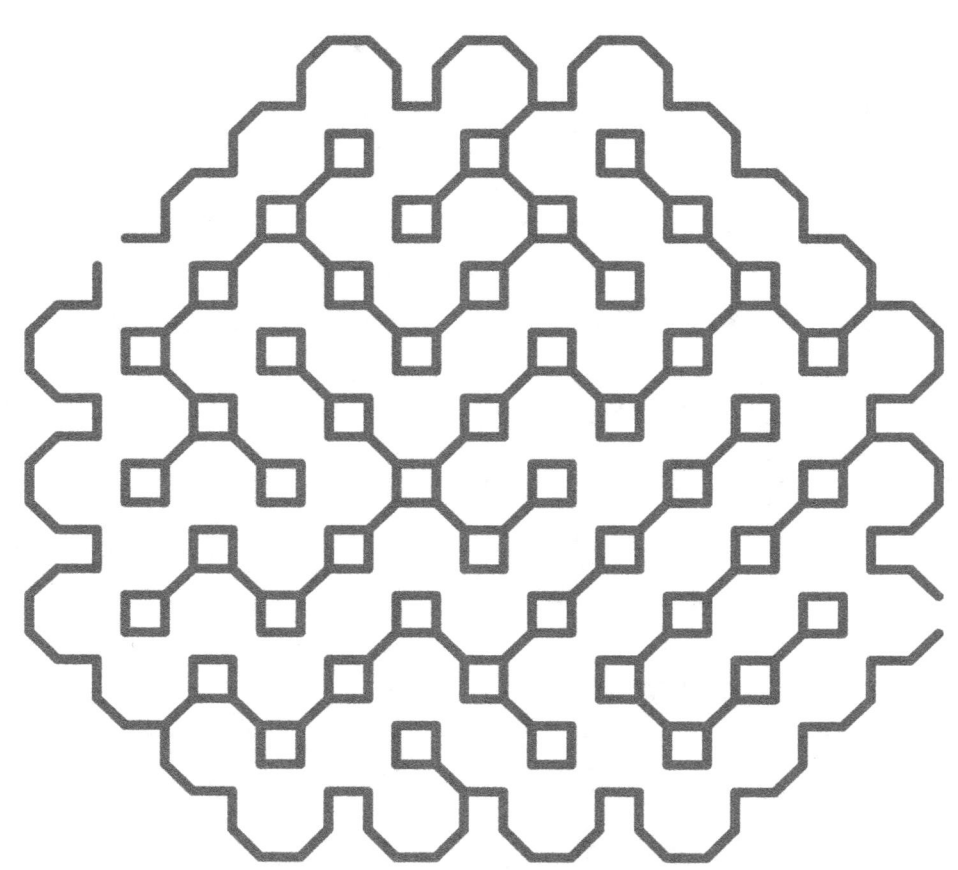

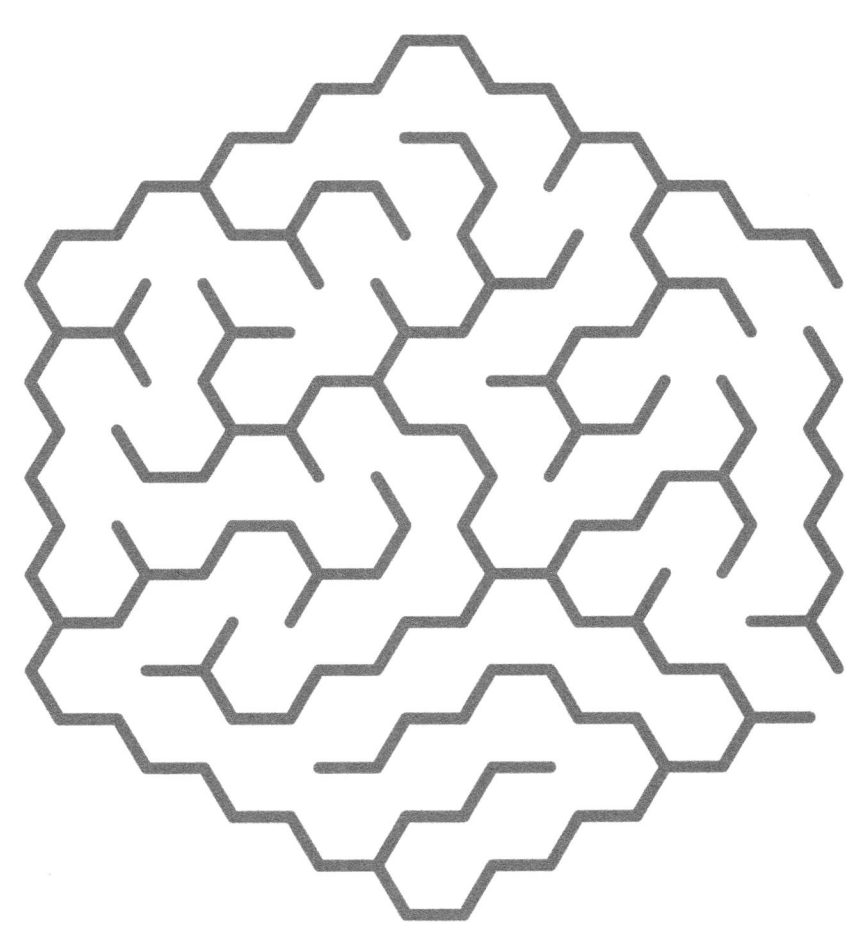

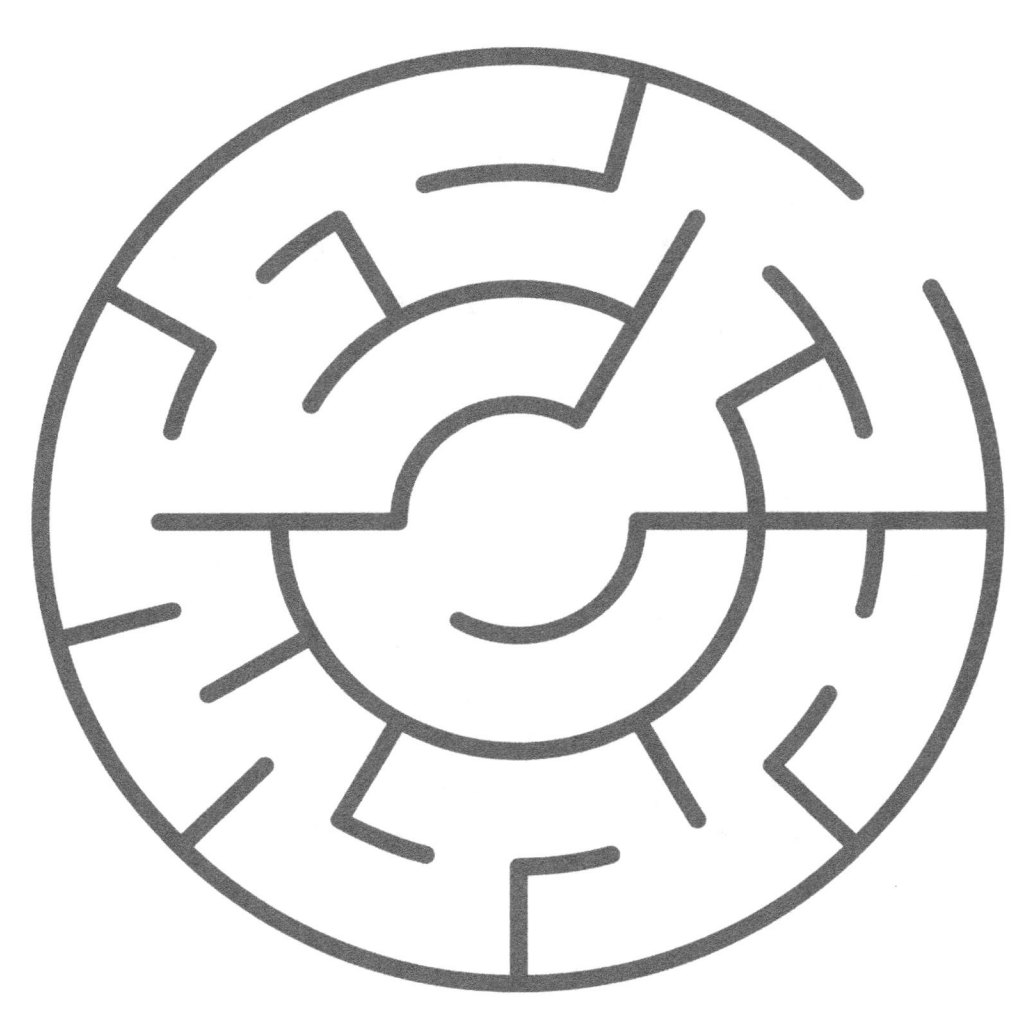

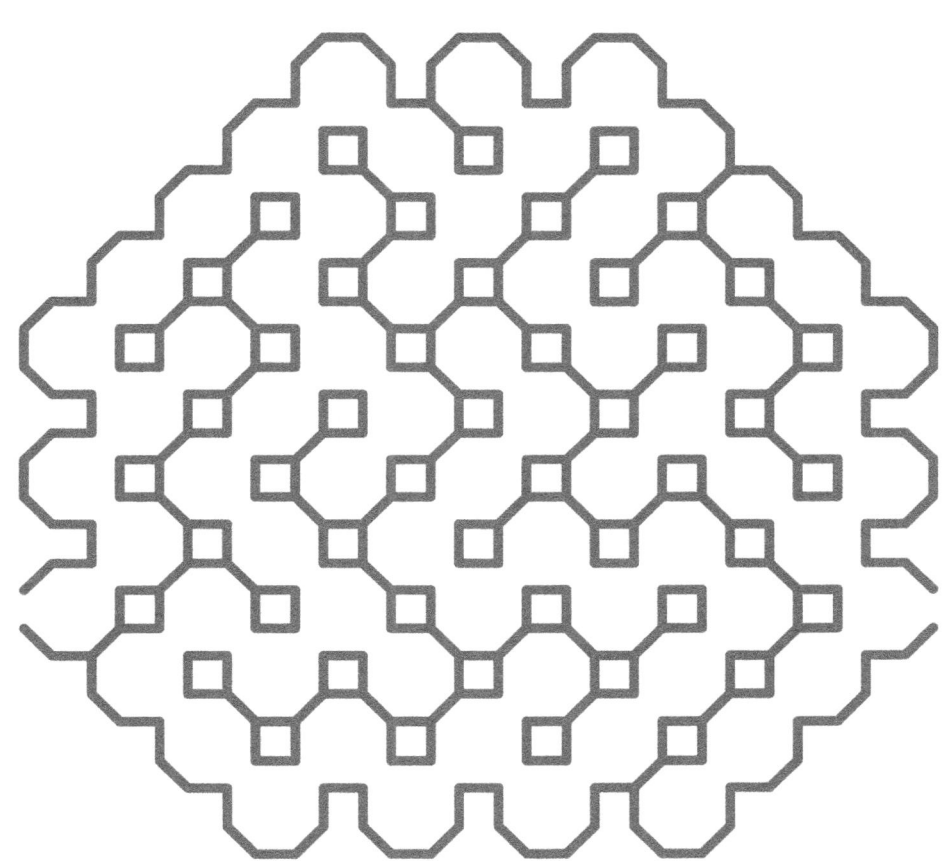

Page 103-1

Page 104-1

Page 105-1

Page 106-1

Page 218   Page 107-1

Page 108-1

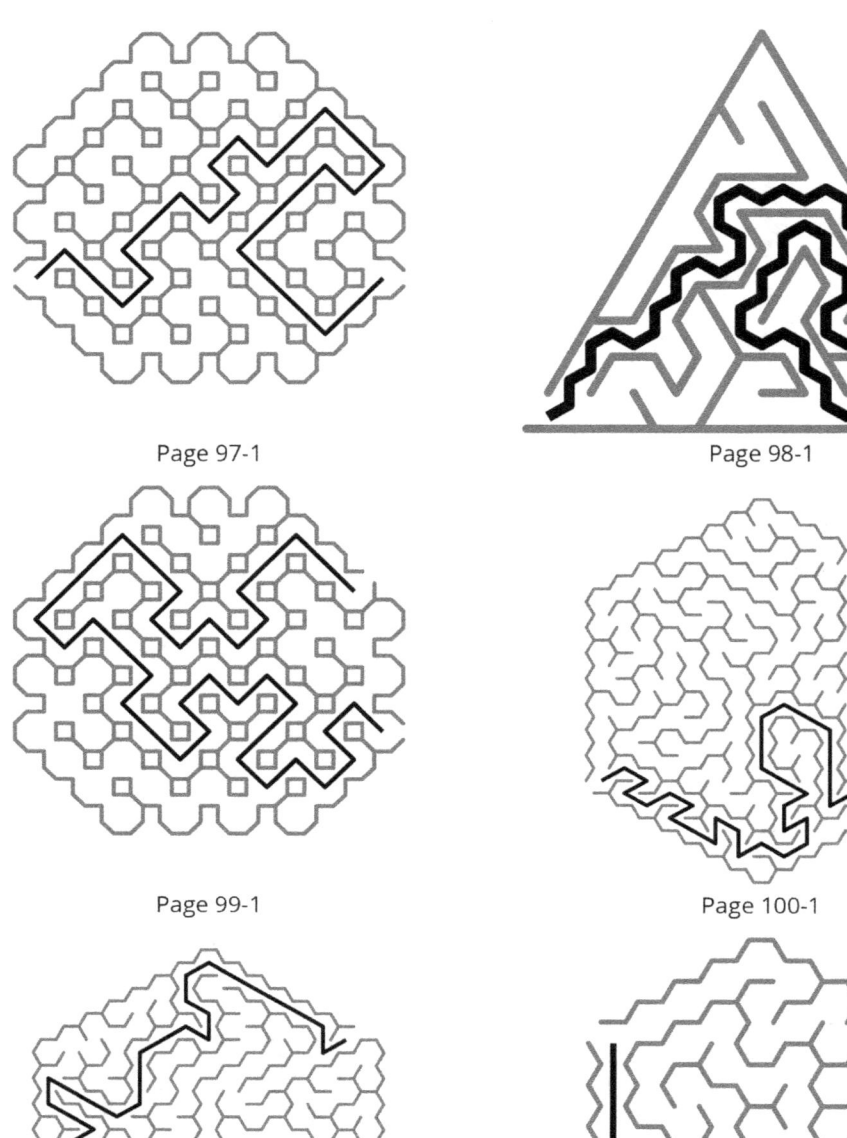

Page 97-1

Page 98-1

Page 99-1

Page 100-1

Page 101-1

Page 102-1

Page 217

Page 109-1

Page 110-1

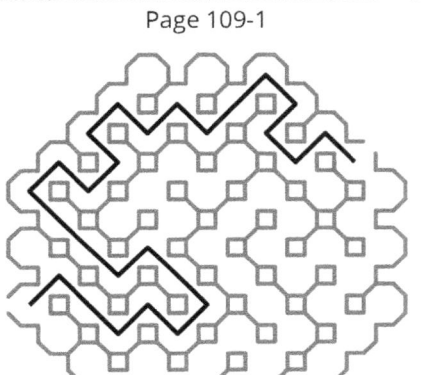
Page 111-1

Page 112-1

Page 113-1

Page 114-1

Page 115-1

Page 116-1

Page 117-1

Page 118-1

Page 220 Page 119-1

Page 120-1

Page 121-1

Page 122-1

Page 123-1

Page 124-1

Page 125-1

Page 126-1

Page 127-1

Page 128-1

Page 129-1

Page 130-1

Page 131-1

Page 132-1

Page 133-1
Page 134-1
Page 135-1
Page 136-1
Page 137-1
Page 138-1
Page 223

Page 139-1

Page 140-1

Page 141-1

Page 142-1

Page 143-1

Page 144-1

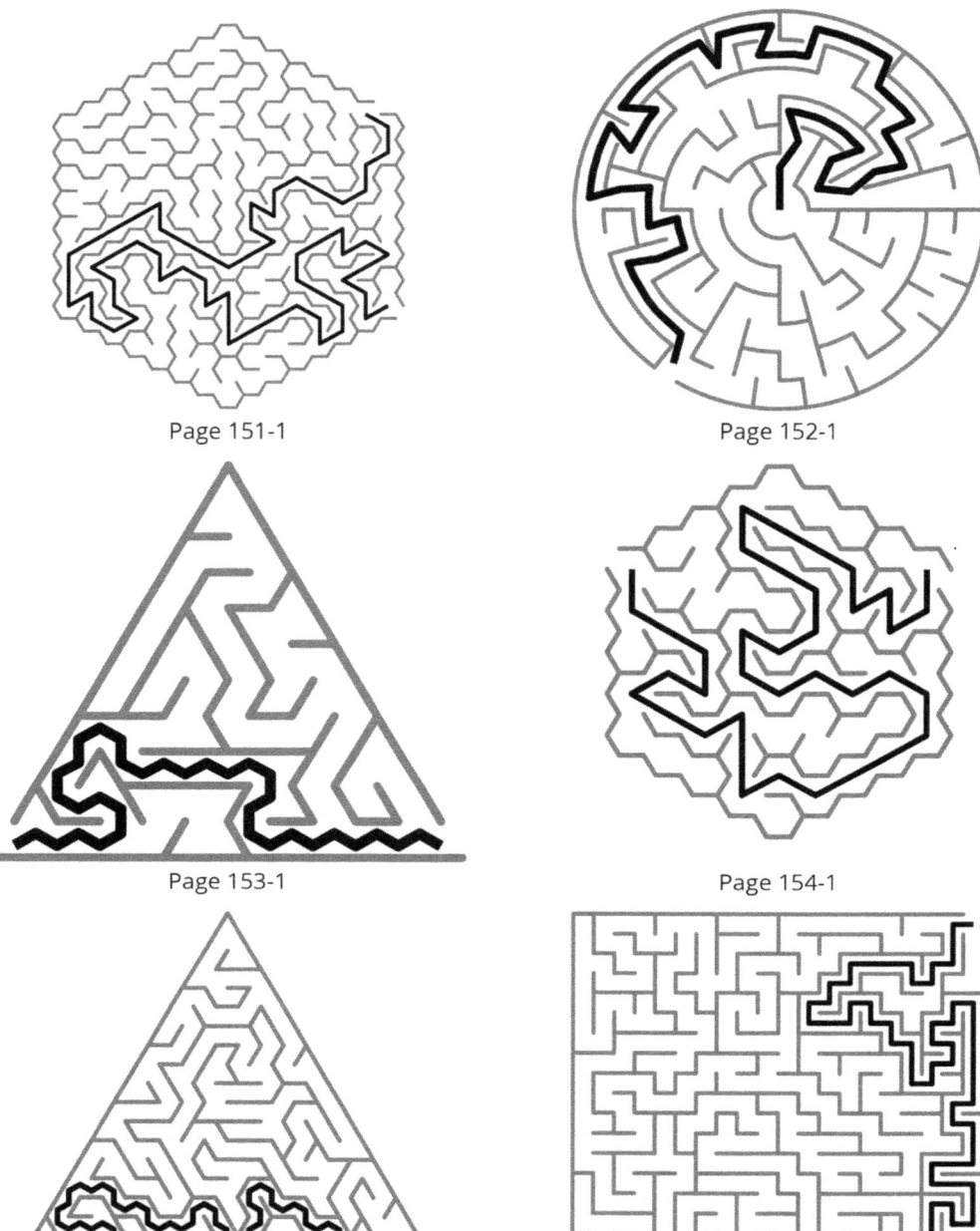

Page 151-1

Page 152-1

Page 153-1

Page 154-1

Page 226   Page 155-1

Page 156-1

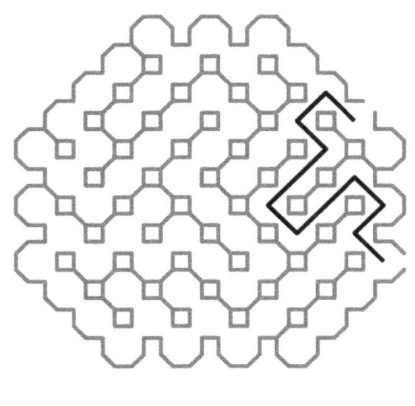

Page 157-1

Page 158-1

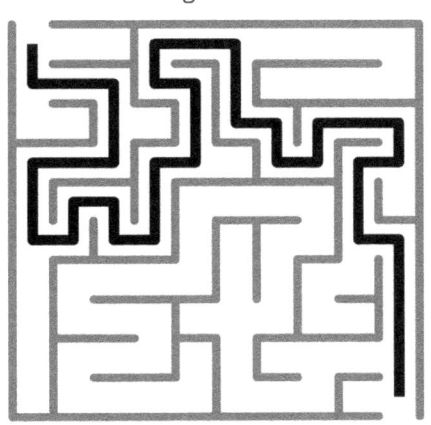

Page 159-1

Page 160-1

Page 161-1

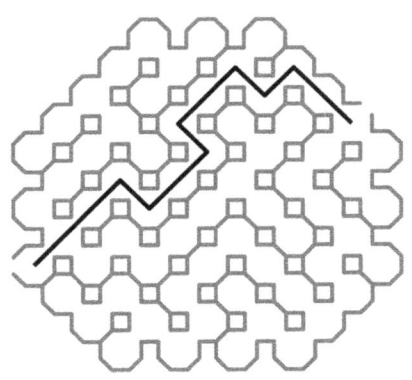

Page 162-1

Page 228   Page 167-1

Page 169-1

Page 170-1

Page 171-1

Page 172-1

Page 173-1

Page 174-1

Page 229

Page 175-1
Page 176-1
Page 177-1
Page 178-1
Page 230
Page 179-1
Page 180-1

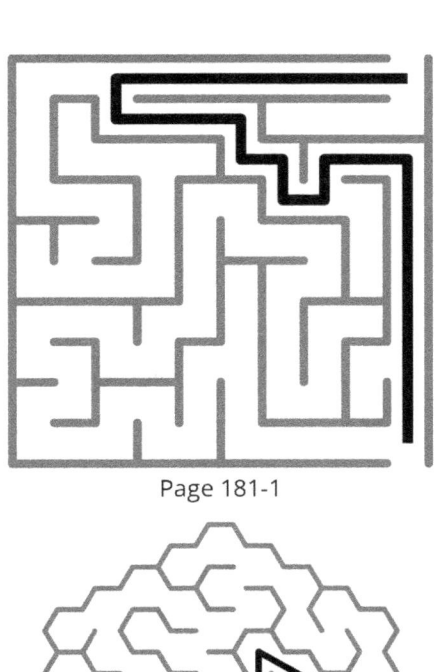

Page 181-1

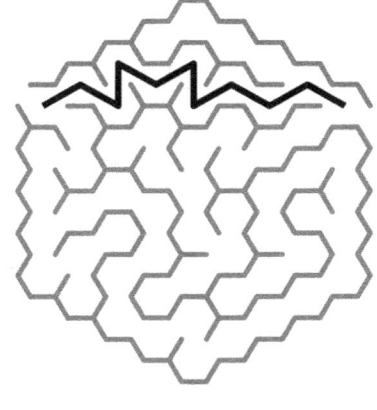

Page 182-1

Page 183-1

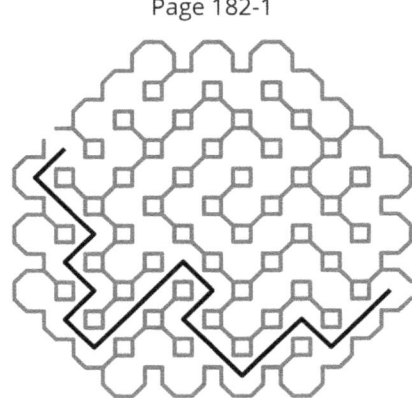

Page 184-1

Page 185-1

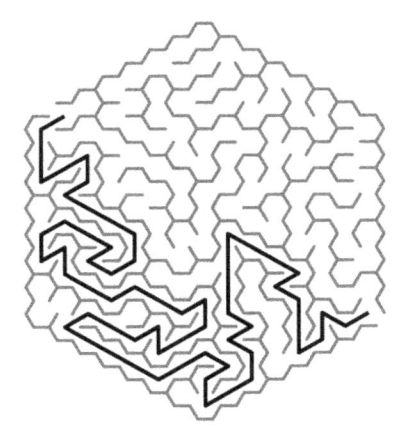

Page 186-1

Page 231

Page 187-1

Page 188-1

Page 189-1

Page 190-1

Page 232   Page 191-1

Page 192-1

Page 193-1

Page 194-1

Page 195-1

Page 196-1

Page 197-1

Page 198-1

Page 233

Page 199-1

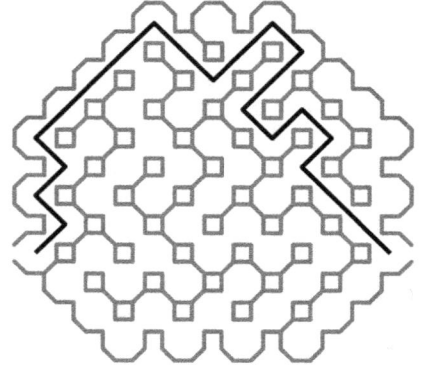

Page 200-1

Page 234

www.ingramcontent.com/pod-product-compliance
Lightning Source LLC
LaVergne TN
LVHW060207080526
838202LV00052B/4205